KEEPING YOUR OWN POULTRY

A practical guide for householders and smallholders, explaining all aspects of keeping a small flock of hens, ducks or geese.

KEEPING YOUR OWN POULTRY

Advice for the Small-scale Beginner

by
Peter Laud
Illustrations by Peter Averis

THORSONS PUBLISHERS LIMITED
Wellingborough, Northamptonshire

First published February 1982
Second Impression August 1982
Third Impression 1984

British Library Cataloguing in Publication Data

Laud, Peter
    Keeping your own poultry.
    1. Poultry—Amateur's manual
    1. Title
    636.5'08'3   SF487

    ISBN 0-7225-0712-7

Printed and bound in Great Britain.

CONTENTS

INTRODUCTION

What is the point of keeping hens at all when supermarkets have a guaranteed supply of eggs packed in neat little plastic containers? What could be simpler than paying money in exchange for a dozen best-battery eggs? No fuss, no bother, no muck on your boots.

Much the same argument can be applied to growing produce in suburban back gardens. Why not leave vegetables to the farmers with their fields, fertilizers and machinery, and eggs to the big commercial undertakings? Surely they are the most efficient? On cost grounds, perhaps, but whether the businessman who keeps his hens in huge factory-like sheds equipped with cages, plastic nipple drinkers and artificial sunlight is one hundred per cent efficient at keeping his hens happy is another matter.

That is not to suggest that big business is necessarily bad, or that we should all revert to being a nation of peasant farmers scraping a living from the soil. The pendulum has swung too far for that. We have left the land and gone into the office, factory and commuter suburb. We have become used to the supermarket and food that comes in plastic prisons.

Yet, despite that, or maybe because of it, many people still yearn for the idea of two-acres-and-a-cow and the 'simple life' (which in practice may be anything but simple) rather than a nine-to-five job in a factory or office block.

Some people actually take the plunge, swapping regular salary cheques and the comforts of suburbia for a place in the country and a part-time job to keep the wolf from the door. Most, however, remain in the cities anchored by the mortgage, security, friends and a whole host of other perfectly valid reasons.

In this age of giant multi-national companies and food that comes pre-packaged and date-stamped, the idea of at least partial self-sufficiency lives on in back gardens up and down the country. Why else would thousands of householders have a vegetable plot? Why else would local authorities in some areas have long waiting lists for people wishing to work allotments... Why else does the well-off executive spend part of his weekend leisure hours tending his potatoes, cabbages, beans and other vegetables? Does he do it for cost reasons? Hardly, for if he cared to cost out his digging time at his hourly rate the produce on offer at the local greengrocer's would represent a positive bargain. Anyone who has grown a hundredweight of potatoes in his back garden knows how much work is involved.

So, why bother growing your own vegetables or producing your own eggs if you can afford to buy both in the High Street? That depends on what value you place on fresh, home-produced food; and what could be fresher than a newly-lifted potato or a hen's egg still warm from the nest? It depends on other things too – like satisfaction and enjoyment. It is satisfying to be able to escape from beneath the umbrella of the giant food companies and the supermarkets and to plough your own furrow. It brings with it a feeling of having beaten a little bit of the system.

There is no scientific evidence of any nutritional difference between a commercially-produced battery egg and one from hens kept free-range or semi-intensively in the back garden. But your own eggs will look and taste different and they will certainly be fresher. Even with slick marketing and high-speed deliveries it still takes a few days for battery eggs to reach the supermarket shelves; and hen eggs are best used as fresh as possible.

Your own eggs should be cheaper too, although any cost savings should be considered a bonus rather than the main aim. No-one is ever going to make a fortune out of keeping six or a dozen hens on a smallholding or in the back garden. If you want to set up your own mini-battery system in a back garden shed with hens in wire cages unable to scratch for food or flap their wings in comfort then this book is not for you. Hens do not need much space. They *can* live in cages. They can – and do – lay eggs in vast numbers while in their wire prisons. But why not, in return for the eggs, give them good and decent lives too?

They *are* ways of producing your own eggs and keeping hens happy at the same time. Think about it though before you start. If you do not want to be bothered with collecting eggs and feeding hens daily; if you object to getting dirty occasionally; if you regard the noise of an excited hen that has just laid (or the crow of a cockerel) as a nuisance and an invasion of privacy then keeping poultry is not for you. The whole point of any hobby is to derive a measure of enjoyment, and if you think that you and a small flock of hens can rub along in a happy relationship, then go ahead.

The routine jobs should be part of the enjoyment and not a daily drudge to be suffered as part of the penalty for keeping your own hens. How much time is involved will depend on the scale of the exercise, but keeping, say, six hens in a back garden run should not take up more than five or ten minutes each day in feeding, collecting eggs and generally enjoying the sight of your own hens. At other times there will be many other jobs as well like repairing the house and wire run, clearing away manure – a useful by-product of your own hens – checking birds that might look off-colour, creosoting woodwork, and so on. The amount of time to be spent on such tasks will depend on the individual's approach but it is a fairly safe bet that extra time spent will yield better dividends.

Hens are hardy creatures. Kept in a ramshackle tin hut encrusted with manure alongside a muddy run and fed a poor diet of the cheapest wheat and household scraps they will still lay some eggs – but not many. Kept in good, clean conditions and fed the right food they will lay far more and the object of the exercise is, after all, plenty of eggs. The hens will also be healthier and happier and those are not bad additional objectives to aim for.

1

BEATING THE BATTERIES

The truth is that most laying hens in the United Kingdom have never seen a growing blade of grass or felt the warmth of natural sunlight. About 95 per cent of all laying hens in the U.K. and 85 per cent of the total E.E.C. flock are confined to battery cages – sometimes three or four to a cage.

Laying hens have developed from jungle fowl – small birds used to the soft earth and warm temperatures of the jungle and the freedom to perch on trees and to forage for food. Today's hen batteries – huge, often windowless buildings – are a world away from free-ranging in the jungle or anywhere else, and the birds live surrounded by labour-saving, cost-cutting gadgetry. There are plastic nipple drinkers for water, drip-trays, pre-mixed high protein food dispensed automatically in carefully measured amounts and their new-laid eggs roll away onto wire shelving for easy collection.

Sunlight is an essential ingredient in the egg-making process of the hen and in batteries it is provided artificially by overhead lighting operated on time switches to control the length of each unnatural day. Every aspect of the hen's life in the battery is controlled for maximum production.

The hens themselves are far removed from their jungle forbears. The ancestor of the domestic fowl of today laid just as many eggs as she chose to sit on – perhaps a dozen – and then she stopped and hatched her brood. She did this twice a year in the spring and late summer and was quite happy with her yearly production of 25-30 eggs. That may have been fine for her but it wasn't enough to satisfy the demands of *homo sapiens* once he had discovered the delights of a boiled egg.

The Battery System

The Hybrid Hen

Years of genetic research and breeding has produced today's modern commercial hen – the hybrid. Hybrids go under a variety of commercial names and numbers but their mission in life is identical: to lay the maximum number of eggs for the minimum input of food in the smallest possible space. Space is one of the main advantages that the battery system has over alternatives because it saves valuable agricultural land for other purposes.

Some hybrids lay up to 300 eggs in the first twelve-month laying season. Production in the second year may be 20 or 25 per cent less and after this their useful commercial life is over and they are then discarded (culled) and a fresh batch of replacements bought in to keep the egg factories in constant production. Some battery birds are culled after only a twelve-month lay.

Hybrids are egg-laying machines; no more, no less. In the battery, just as in all other agricultural enterprises, costs and efficiency are uppermost, and without a doubt batteries turn out the cheapest eggs for the mass market.

However, despite soothing words from the barons of the battery business and the farm unions, the controversy over cages, which came into use in the U.K. in the early 1950s, continues unabated. Critics claim that life in the cages represents gross deprivation and possible cruelty. It is claimed that boredom leads to hens pecking each other's feathers, cannibalism, disease and death.

There have been frequent calls for a total ban on the cage system, and attempts have been made to bring the lifestyle of the battery hen into the political arena. Little has happened. The batteries remain and so do the regimented rows of caged birds.

The pro-battery lobby believes that the argument is stronger on emotion than fact. This is what the National Farmers Union of England and Wales has to say:

> The cost of keeping hens on free range is just about double that of keeping them in batteries. The higher prices which would result would put eggs beyond the pocket of many consumers and would be particularly hard upon the lower income group families and old people who rely upon eggs as a major source of protein.
>
> Egg prices have fallen by nearly 50 per cent since the early 1950s. This is primarily due to the efficiency of the battery cage system which has produced ample supplies of high quality eggs. Abolition of the battery cage would set the industry and the consumer back a full twenty years.

Chickens Lib, the pressure group campaigning for batteries to be outlawed, says:

> Disease spreads like wildfire in the intensive conditions of the battery house. If domestic animals were kept in comparable conditions their owners would be prosecuted for cruelty.

The argument goes on and there is recognition among some Ministry of Agriculture experts that battery cages may not provide an ideal environment for the laying hen. What are the commercial alternatives?

The Deep-Litter System

The deep-litter system accounts for 2.2 per cent of the 50 million bird laying flock in the U.K. In this system the birds are still housed in large, again often windowless buildings, but are free to move around rather than being restricted to cages.

The Deep-Litter System

The house floors are covered with a deep layer of wood shavings, or a mixture of shavings and chopped straw which is known as 'litter' – hence the term 'deep litter'. Labour-saving devices for feed and water are used together with artificial lighting, but the inmates do have a certain degree of freedom. It is not ideal but many would argue that it is better than the battery cage.

The problem is that deep-litter produced eggs cost more than those from battery systems. With automatic equipment one man can tend up to 6,000 birds on a deep litter; in the battery he can look after five times as many.

There are other disadvantages too. One is the problem of keeping the temperature of the housing right. If it becomes either too hot or too cold egg production falls off, which is why batteries are kept at an even temperature of around 75°F/24°C. In deep litter systems some of the eggs may become dirty, cracked or even lost. Disease and cannibalism can also break out and there is competition between the hens for food.

It is claimed that nearly £300 million worth of new housing and equipment would be needed if deep litter systems were to replace battery cages.

Free-Range

Another alternative is to keep commercial flocks free-range with static or portable houses for perching and laying, and giving access to large grassed areas during the day. The maximum commercial stocking rate is about 180 birds to the acre. But, on free-range, egg production is lower and production costs are again higher than in batteries.

Some hens are also kept in fold units which are small houses with grass runs attached. The runs are moved daily to prevent the ground becoming 'chicken sick' and diseased. There is also a compromise system called a hen-yard which involves a house or a covered pen attached to an adjoining straw-covered yard two or three times as big.

Commercially the batteries reign supreme and are likely to continue to do so because of low production costs. In a Ministry of Agriculture survey of the major systems for 1979-80 the annual egg yield per battery bird was 252 compared with 229 in deep litter and 197 for free range.

Multi-level Aviaries

Research is under way, however, into multi-level aviaries, a housing system where the hens are free to move from one platform to another via ladders – a sort of high-rise flat for hens.

This gives the birds the freedom to choose their own nesting sites and to scratch in litter, both of which are very natural activities for the hen. Certainly aviaries might provide a far better lifestyle for the hen but whether they will prove a satisfactory commercial alternative to the battery remains to be seen.

The eggs may end up costing more than they do on deep litter and free-range systems and the question is, would the average housewife pay the extra just to give a laying hen a better quality of life? That must surely be in some doubt. Costs rule the family budget just as they do in the battery business. The truth is that many housewives probably don't care where the eggs come from or under what conditions as long as the price is right.

But, if you harbour a sneaking suspicion that it is wrong for a hen to be confined in a cage; if you believe that chickens have certain rights too (and why not?) then where do you get your eggs from?

Buying Free-Range Eggs
You *can* hunt around for a farmer selling free-range eggs and pay extra for them. Truly free-range eggs normally command a price premium. But do not be conned into thinking that a sign saying 'farm fresh eggs' is necessarily a guarantee of free-range hens. The farmer might have a small battery of his own or be buying in from a local battery for re-sale. Use your eyes and see if you can see any hens wandering around the place.

The real solution is to become a domestic poultryman yourself. The responsibility may seem awesome but it need not be a burden. The enjoyment derived from this worthwhile hobby is good for you, and so are the eggs.

Eggs are one of the perfect foods containing all the ingredients of a good diet: body building materials such as proteins and mineral trace elements; fats and traces of carbohydrate which produce the energy necessary for growth; vitamins for the efficient use of nutrients in the body. An egg contains 12 per cent protein, 10.5 per cent fat and 11.8 per cent minerals, vitamins and carbohydrates. The rest is water.

An average-sized egg contains about 85 calories, and the quality of egg protein is so high that it is used by nutritionists as the standard against which most other forms of protein are judged.

All this goodness comes in its own protective package. It has been calculated that for thickness and strength an egg shell is stronger than the most sophisticated concrete building. Try breaking a perfectly sound, uncracked shell by exerting hand pressure on the two ends and you will get some idea of how strong the shell is.

Brown Eggs versus White

While on the subject of egg shells we can be rid of the nonsense spoken about brown- and white-shelled eggs. Shell colour varies according to the breed of hen laying the egg. Today's hybrids have been developed in the main from two traditional breeds. Those that lay brown-shelled eggs are derived from the Rhode Island Red and those that lay white from the White Leghorn.

Despite the colour prejudice, which has caused some supermarkets to stop selling white-shelled eggs altogether, there is not a scrap of difference in nutritional value between the two. Psychologists say that the colour brown conjures up in the mind of the buyer pictures of rolling countryside and free-range hens which may be a nice cosy thought, but if the eggs are from a supermarket it is most likely that the hens that laid them won't have seen a square inch of countryside in their lives.

Neither is there much nutritional significance in the colour of the yolk. Variations in yolk colour are the result largely of the food the hen has eaten. Commercial producers have to ensure that the diet of hens has sufficient pigmentation to achieve this, but for the domestic poultryman feeding the hens some maize and plenty of greenstuffs (carrot too) will produce eggs with a rich, yellow yolk. And while this may not necessarily be better nutritionally it certainly looks healthier than a pale, anaemic-looking yolk.

Size of Flock

How many hens to start with? That really depends on how large the family is, but six well-managed hens will keep the average family of four in eggs throughout the year. Each hen should produce around 200 eggs, maybe more, in her first laying season and slightly fewer in the second. Before starting, though, check two points. Make sure that there are no local by-laws restricting householders from keeping domestic poultry. Do this by contacting the environmental health department at your local council. And remember that keeping even half a dozen hens is a seven day a week job. The daily tasks might take only a few minutes but they still have to be done, so it is important that you have a friendly neighbour who can take over if you want to go away for a weekend or holiday. You can always pay him back in fresh eggs.

Maximizing Production

There are certain essentials for achieving maximum production and I make no apologies if that sounds a bit like the terminology of the battery business. Domestic hens have got to pay their way just like their caged counterparts but, unlike the battery hen, birds kept in a back garden run or free-range on a smallholding can also enjoy a good life, free to feel the sun's warmth and take daily baths in the dust. These key points are:

First-class pullets which have been bred to lay. A pullet is a female chicken in its first full year of laying.

Correct feeding. No bird is going to lay many eggs on household scraps and whatever she can find for herself, not even a totally free-range hen able to wander wherever the fancy takes her. The domestic hen has been bred to lay and lay well, but to do this she needs high protein food. This will mean buying in proprietary food and supplementing this with your own garden produce. Other essentials of a good diet are grit and a fresh supply of clean water.

Good Housing. This is not as vital as might be supposed but a henhouse that is proofed against the weather, foxes, rats, mice, cats and dogs certainly helps. For the suburban dweller this means some kind of house with one or two runs attached or even a movable fold unit. The smallholder with a free-range flock, or one with access to large grassed areas, may be able to convert an existing building as long as it is dry and free of draughts.

Housing for hens need not be palatial, but they do need somewhere to dodge the worst of the weather because, unlike ducks, they do not have the benefit of oiled feathers. They also need a place to lay eggs where you can find them. The housing needs to be sited correctly and kept clean, and management of the run or runs in a back garden system is just as important. Hens will not remain healthy if kept confined to the same muddy run day after day. They also get bored, which is exactly what the domestic poultryman is seeking to avoid in his stock. Boredom belongs to the battery.

How Long Can You Keep Hens For?

In theory, as long as you like, but after a couple of years you will be keeping them rather than the other way round. It is not generally worthwhile keeping hens after they have completed their second year's lay. Production – 20-25 per cent down in the second year – will drop further in later years although the eggs will be larger.

Most suburban poultrymen are tied to buying in food for their hens, and rising food costs and lower returns is a state of affairs that does not make much sense. If you do not mind paying the feed bill and you feel magnanimous towards your hens then by all means keep them until they are pensioners. They will be grateful for having escaped the casserole.

For most people though this idea of running a home for geriatric hens is a non-starter. The most economical plan is to clear the hens out after two years and start afresh with new birds aged about 16-18 weeks, when they will be on the point of laying their first eggs. It is not a good idea to keep birds of different ages in the same flock. If birds of two age groups are mixed together the chances are the younger bird will get pushed to the back of the queue at the feed trough and the older bird may get too fat – and unhealthy as a result.

The problem of getting rid of the old hens is usually the family attachment, especially if there are children in the household. Most likely they will have pet names. You might be able to sell the birds or find someone who is willing to incorporate them into a flock of similar aged hens, but if not then wring their necks and put them in the casserole which is the fate of all old hens too tough to be roasted in the oven. Whether you let on to your children that you are having casseroled Henrietta or Matilda for lunch is entirely up to you.

You don't need to have a cockerel around the place for your hens to lay eggs. The only point of keeping a cockerel is to have a supply of fertile eggs for hatching out replacement Henriettas.

2

HOUSING

The type of housing system to be used will be determined to a large extent by the amount of space available. Without doubt the most natural (although not perhaps the most profitable) way to keep hens is to have them on a truly free-range system where they are able to wander anywhere they choose – except into the vegetable garden which they will peck to pieces in no time. Hens are quite unable to distinguish between, say, cabbages of which you might have plenty and sprouts which might be in very short supply.

Free-range hens are fine for the smallholder with a few acres, but this system is obviously out of the question for the suburban poultryman. The average-sized back garden provides nothing like enough room, and the neighbours just might object to your hens breaking into their gardens and making off with their soft fruit.

So the flock will have to be kept restricted in some sort of housing with access to an outside wire run or, better still, two runs. There is nothing wrong with this, and provided certain minimum space requirements are borne in mind the hens will lead happy, healthy and productive lives.

Housing Systems
Possible systems include: a permanently-sited house with two, or even three, runs attached provided there is enough space in the garden; a moveable house and run which can be carried to fresh ground when necessary, known as a fold unit; a hen-pen which, like the fold unit, is an all-in-one system providing roosting and scratching areas which may be the answer if space is severely limited; a covered run and perching area built as a lean-to against a wall as a small-scale adaptation of the commercial hen yard.

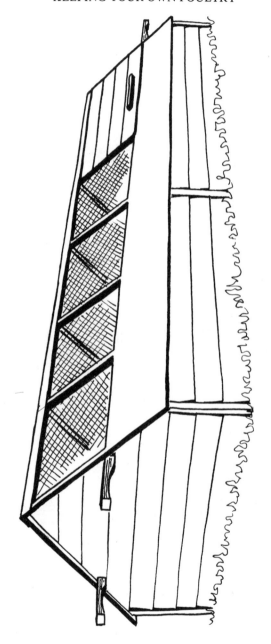

Example of a moveable fold unit

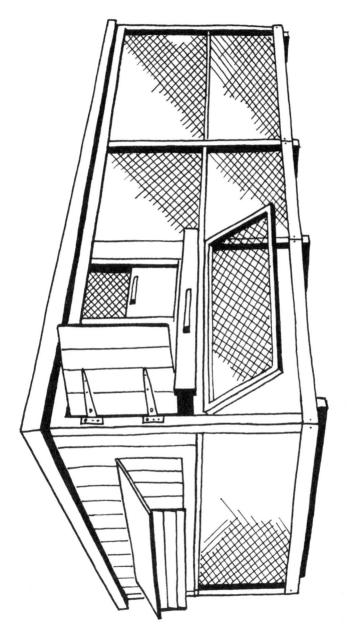

Poultry pen for use where space is limited

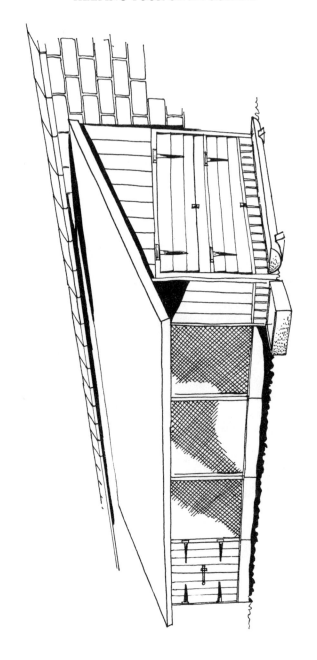

Poultry house (using existing garden wall)

These are suggestions only. It is rare to find two do-it-yourself systems exactly the same, and adaptations and improvements are always possible. Back garden poultry-keeping is, by definition, a system that is controlled and restricted but that does not mean the birds will suffer the deprivations and artificiality of the battery house.

The manufacture of hen houses has become a sizeable industry, growing with the movement towards at least partial self-sufficiency in suburbia, and most types of housing can be bought. They are normally delivered in sections for home erection. Costs of ready-made housing vary, but at the present time a house and run for six pullets costs about £110-£125, and a fold unit for a dozen birds about the same, although, like everything else, these costs tend to rise.

The capital cost of setting up the venture might seem high, but a house that is well-maintained will keep its value when the time comes to dispose of it. You may of course be able to acquire good second-hand housing at a farm auction and improve it if necessary with common sense and a spot of do-it-yourself. Second-hand housing should be given a thorough clean through before you put your own stock in.

Whatever you buy, whether new or second-hand, make sure it is capable of withstanding all the vagaries of the British climate. Remember, it has got to sit outside day after day in wind, rain, frost, snow and sunlight, so avoid cheap and flimsy housing. Cutting corners at the outset is a bad policy.

If you have access to good second-hand timber you might consider making your own hen house. Contact other poultry keepers in the area, study their methods, pinch a few ideas and work out your own housing compromise. Most domestic poultrymen do not mind sharing their secrets.

The essentials of a good house are that it is dry and well-ventilated, but without draughts, and that it provides sufficient space for each bird. Aim to provide 2-3 sq ft of floor space for each bird in the house and, if that sounds somewhat inadequate, consider that in battery systems a cage measuring 15 in x 19 in sometimes accomodates two or three hens!

The do-it-yourself enthusiast with one eye on economy might be tempted to build chicken housing of second-hand corrugated iron sheets on a timber framework. The appearance of sheeting can be improved with green or black metal preservative paint but the real snag with iron is that in summer it may get too hot, even at night through heat retention, and in winter may be too cold. Hens do not like severe changes in temperature. The problem can be partly overcome by lining the sheets with matchboard, chipboard or hardboard leaving an inch or two of air space. A layer of roofing felt between the lining and the iron helps insulation and prevents leaks in wet weather. Nail holes in second-hand sheets can be plugged with mastic available from ironmongers or builder's merchants.

Permanent Housing

A garden shed measuring 6 ft x 4 ft is fine for six or eight hens because it is large enough for them to remain indoors in severe weather without the risk of overcrowding. Hens dislike wind, rain and mud just as much as we do. If the shed is high enough to allow standing room this makes cleaning of the interior much easier.

If you are putting up a new shed, then think of the neighbours. They will see it too so avoid putting up some unsightly edifice of rusting tin. Make the place neat and attractive, both for the hens who have to live in it and for humans who have to look at it. Wood is generally the best material for chicken houses.

Another point to bear in mind about size is that you may wish at some stage to expand from, say, six hens to a dozen so the bigger the shed the better. A small flock of hens will not do well in something the size of a tea chest. Good ventilation without draughts is essential because it reduces the risk of the birds suffering from respiratory diseases. Poor ventilation is indicated by a smell of ammonia when the shed is opened up first thing each morning, and there will be a definite 'fug' instead of fresh air.

Good ready-made housing is provided with adequate vents to overcome this, often in the form of wire mesh 'windows', and these will have to be included when building from scratch or converting and existing garden shed. Sometimes wooden shutters are also provided to block off the wire vents in windy weather. Clear plastic can be used for windows. It is cheaper than glass, cuts easier and is simpler to use than glass. And, when broken, is less of a risk to hens and humans.

Siting the House

Just as important as good ventilation is the correct siting of the house. The hen is stimulated into laying by the amount of daylight falling on her eyes, so ideally windows should be at the front facing south-east to get the most daylight early in the morning with the back of the house providing protection from north-west winds in winter. If the prevailing storms are from the west the house should face east.

There are other considerations when siting the shed too. Even in the best managed system there is a risk of smells, especially in warm weather, although regular cleaning once a week will go a long way towards avoiding this. Site the house where winds will not carry any smell towards houses, either your own or your neighbour's. If the garden slopes, site the house at the top or even half way down, but not at the bottom because this could make the run permanently muddy in wet weather.

The roof of the house should extend at least three inches over the sides to throw off rain. It is better still to run the rainwater off in guttering to a water butt where it can be stored for use in the garden later.

When covering a roof in roofing felt fasten it with strips of wood about 2 in x $\frac{3}{8}$ in, nailing through both the wood and the felt into the roof timbers. Fastened with felt nails only, the felt may crack and rip in windy weather.

Flooring

Ready-made housing normally has solid wooden floors, either of tongue-and-groove timber or straight-edged planks. If you are making your own floor make sure the boards are a good, close fit and are well creosoted or tarred underneath. Another possibility is a concrete floor and for this a good foundation of hardcore is essential, and a damp-proof membrane (such as old plastic fertilizer bags laid over the hardcore and overlapping each other by two or three inches) will stop any damp rising through the floor. Hens like to keep their feet dry.

Ask a local builder for advice on mixing concrete for floors – generally a mix of four parts of $\frac{1}{2}$ in gravel, two of sand and one of cement will do. For a really flat surface, which may help when cleaning the shed out, put on top an inch of concrete made of sand (or granite dust) and cement in a ratio of about six to one.

It might be worth hiring a concrete mixer for a day if you are putting down a large floor area – 8 ft x 6 ft may not look very large, but wait until you start hand-mixing and laying the concrete.

Concrete makes a durable floor and stops rats gnawing into the house from underneath, but it is a cold material and so requires a good depth of litter – wood shavings, sawdust, peat moss, chopped straw (preferably barley which breaks down better than wheat) or even dry autumn leaves and dry bracken fern. Avoid using hay because it tends to hold the wet, and leads to mouldy litter. Another drawback is that hay does not rot down as quickly as straw on the compost or dung heap.

Flooring can also be made of wooden slats, wire, or gravel and rubble rammed well down. Slatted floors allow some of the chicken droppings to fall through for clearing out later and also help in ventilating the house. For a rammed floor remove the surface soil to a depth of about 6 in and fill with gravel, brick ends, and rubble, and pound the lot down either with a hand rammer or a powered rammer (obtained at most good hire shops).

Rammed floors still require litter, as do concrete and timber floors, but if the garden is low lying then they are best avoided because of the problem of rising damp. When making your own house, or re-furbishing a second-hand one, creosote the inside, especially the corners and crevices where blood-sucking insects like the red mite can gather. Those will do your hens absolutely no good at all. Treat any suspect timber for woodworm too, but make sure that the vapours from the woodworm solution have cleared before putting the hens in. Creosote or paint the outside of the house and keep it looking smart. Unsightly housing and muddy runs containing a few damp and dishevelled hens do nothing for the cause of back garden poultry-keeping.

Interior Fittings

Hens roost at night on perches, and the height of these is important because if they are too high the birds might injure their legs and feet when alighting in the morning. Fix the perches about 18 in to 2 ft from the floor in sockets on either side of the house to allow easy removal for cleaning. Do not nail them permanently into place. Allow about 8 in of perch space for each bird and, if more than one perch is needed, fix the next about

20 in away at the same height.

Perches are best made of timber 2-3 in wide with the sharp edges rounded off so the hens can get a good grip. In their natural state hens roosted in trees (some still do given the chance) but it is a mistake to use branches as perches in the belief that the hens are getting a touch of true life. Branches with the bark on cause problems because when the wood dries out the hollow between wood and bark provides a perfect home for minute parasites which live off hens. Another snag is that uneven perches made of branches are difficult to clean, so why give yourself bruised knuckles and extra work?

About half the droppings of a hen are deposited while the bird is roosting so a board about 18 in wide placed 8 in to 9 in below each perch makes cleaning much easier. The droppings board can then be scraped off into a bucket once a week and the job is made easier if each board is sprinkled after scraping with sawdust or sand to keep the droppings dry. Moist droppings lose their nitrogen content quicker than dry droppings and it is the nitrogen content in the manure which makes it so valuable to the gardener.

Nest boxes – the containers in which the hens lay their eggs – can be either built onto the house with a separate lid so that the eggs can be collected without having to enter the house or they can be placed in the house itself.

Nest boxes are best placed in the darkest part of the house and one box measuring 10 in x 12 in x 12 in should be provided for every three hens, although since hens are sociable when it comes to nesting, two or even three may decide to lay in the same box at the same time if it is large enough. Darkness is important because it stops hens eating their own eggs and also prevents any attacks on a laying hen. When laying, the area around the hen's vent (through which the completed egg is laid) becomes slightly red and in confined circumstances this can encourage other hens to peck it. Many problems in poultry-keeping arise from having too many hens in too small a space.

Egg eating – which is often partly a result of overcrowding and boredom among the hens – is an annoying habit and can prove costly for the small-scale poultryman. In batteries, new laid eggs roll away out of reach of the hens, but the best way for the domestic keeper to overcome the problem is by making sure the nest boxes are dark. This can be achieved by tacking loose strips of sacking or thin carpet, about an inch wide, over the front of the box leaving the material loose at the bottom so the hens can still enter the nest box. A strip of wood at the bottom edge of the box will stop new laid eggs rolling onto the floor of the house and breaking. Broken eggs can often trigger an outbreak of egg-eating which may be difficult to stop. Nest boxes should be raised a few inches off the floor but not at the same height as the perches or the birds will start sleeping in the boxes and fouling them. Hens will not lay in dirty nesting boxes.

Straw is ideal for making nests warm and inviting, and is better than hay. If you are using wooden boxes as nests do not place them beneath the perches. That will guarantee dirty nests. Also make sure the hen cannot tip the box over while entering and leaving. This will not only damage the eggs but the episode may interrupt the laying pattern. They prefer the quiet life.

A water drinker inside the shed, as well as one outside, is a good idea because it allows the hens to drink before being unlocked each morning. Hens are naturally thirsty creatures and are more likely to die of dehydration than starvation. The drinker can be either of galvanized metal or polythene, and both types are readily available.

Suspend the drinkers a few inches off the ground on wire to stop the birds fouling the water. Do not use old washing up bowls as drinkers because the water will soon become dirty. Fresh, clean water is an essential part of the hen's dietary needs.

No equipment for feeding will normally be needed in the house because it is not good practice to feed hens inside. Left-over food encourages vermin. The only time when the hens will need to be fed indoors is when they are confined for short periods in very bad weather.

The house will need a small door for the hens to get in and out known as a 'pop hole'. This should be about 12 in x 10 in and more than one will be needed to give access to different runs. Sliding doors tend to swell in wet weather so pop holes that hinge at the bottom and can be folded down as hen ramps are better.

The Hen Run

No flock of hens should be confined to the same small grass run day after day. Hens are susceptible to disease picked up off the ground, and confinement in the same run ensures ideal conditions for a build-up of disease.

Two runs, or three if space allows, means that grazing areas can be rotated with one in use and the other being rested. Two small runs are better than one large one. The amount of available space will determine the size of the runs but if possible make them twice the size of the house. A house measuring 6 ft x 4 ft and two runs of 12 ft x 4 ft each would be adequate for six to eight hens. At the very least give each bird 2 or 3 sq ft of run space.

It is possible to get by with one run but this should not be kept as a grassed run because in wet weather it will be a permanent quagmire. Instead dig out an area about twice the size of the house to a depth of 6 in and fill with hardcore topped off with gravel to provide a well-drained scratching area. The house roof can be extended over part or all of the run to provide extra protection against the rain.

The simplest way of making runs is to use 6 ft chicken wire of 1 in or 2 in mesh fastened to posts which have been driven firmly into the ground. Chicken wire stapled directly onto posts tends to break when flexed by wind and is also difficult to remove without a special pair of fencing pliers. Instead, drive the staples into the post first at intervals of 18 in and tie the chicken wire onto the staples with galvanized wire. This makes it much easier to take the chicken wire off if the run has to be moved at a later date.

To keep the chicken wire taut and firm the posts will need to be every 4 or 5 ft and threading heavy gauge galvanized wire through the chicken wire near the bottom, half way up and close to the top, stapling to each post in turn, will help. The posts themselves should be pointed and creosoted and the chicken mesh fixed to the ground with wooden or metal pegs, otherwise the hens will escape underneath. A portable fold unit may be the answer if you have the space – like a paddock or orchard – but frequent moving to fresh ground is essential and this may need to be done two or three times a week, or even daily depending on the amount of grass growth.

Fold units which are moved regularly are a good way of improving poor grassland because the droppings are spread evenly over the whole area. All that is required in practice is to move the unit its own width, slowly rotating it over the whole of the area, although care must be taken not to use the original site too soon. Fold units can be bought − one for twelve pullets presently costs about £150 − but the do-it-yourselfer can make his own, either as an integral unit or with an A-frame house and a separate wire run $2\frac{1}{2}$ to 3 ft high butting up firmly against it. The unit should be strong enough to withstand regular handling and obviously care must be taken to ensure that the unit does not get damaged by other animals grazing the same area.

Free-Range

There are few better sights than a flock of hens with the freedom to wander everywhere at will − except into the garden. This

The Free-Range System

surely is the most natural way of keeping hens and if they do start grazing a neighbour's field he need have no cause for alarm. He will, after all, be getting some fine and free fertilizer. In suburban areas most people are obliged, for space reasons, to adopt a house-and-run system but if you have a smallholding which has an acre or two then complete free-ranging is worth considering.

Commercially flocks on free-range graze each area of land available on a rotational basis to prevent the risk of disease building up. This calls for a great deal of fencing and the term 'free-range' for flocks like that seems a bit of a misnomer. If you have, say, a dozen hens and an acre or two then why not give them the complete freedom of the place?

There are some disadvantages to this. The hens might prefer laying in their own secret nests under a hedge or an old tarpaulin or indeed anywhere rather than the clean warm and inviting nest boxes you have carefully provided. But if you delay unlocking the hens until late morning or mid-day you should not lose too many eggs. Keep an eye on any hen that sprints off after being let out and you should find her secret hideaway. The alternative is to listen out for the clucking of a hen that has just laid (which is fairly distinctive as you will soon discover) and to start searching in the area where the hen is loudly parading. Chances are the nest won't be far away.

Foxes, of course, can be a menace to the free-range flock especially during the winter, and cunning Reynard always seems to take the best. If you have a flock of ten or a dozen hens of which only two or three happen to be in lay they are the ones most likely to disappear. The obvious solution is to get rid of the foxes but that may be easier said than done. They have just as much right to be around as we have. In practice the loss of the odd hen from time to time may be the price you pay for keeping hens free-range.

Another possible problem is that free-range hens can land you in trouble should they break into your neighbour's garden and ruin it. Hens are no respecters of other people's property, especially if the cabbages are greener on the other side of the fence. Not only would a hen raid like that jeopardize friendly relations with your neighbour but he could, if he so wished, take out an action for damages, and the idea of keeping your own hens is to provide fresh, cut-price eggs – not to line the pockets of solicitors.

This problem of hens damaging neighbouring property applies equally to the back garden flock, but if the fencing around the run is good and not full of gaping holes then the hens are unlikely to go 'absent without leave' in the first place. Bear in mind also that if a hen wanders onto a road and gets run over the driver is not obliged to pay compensation. Hens do not have a right of way on a public road and in this respect differ from ducks and geese.

A free-range flock does, inevitably, cause a certain amount of mess so if you want to keep the area around the back door clear of droppings then fence it off in some way. Hens do not mind where they drop their calling cards and seem to have a preference for newly swept concrete yards! In all probability you will end up with a lot of nitrogen exactly where you don't want it.

Some old-school farmers keep a flock of free-range hens often for no other reason that they have always done so and hens look right about the place. Feeding the hens, collecting (and selling) the eggs is often the strict domain of the farmer's wife. But the economics of some free-range flocks on farms do not bear too much scrutiny. Old hens, inadequate badly-ventilated housing and insufficient food all make for poor returns.

To believe that just because the birds are free-range they can somehow live on fresh air, green grass and earwigs is a total myth. The same guidelines on housing apply as before – good ventilation, adequate perching space, inviting nest boxes and regular cleaning. If correctly housed and properly fed a free-range flock can be highly productive.

On a smallholding there may be a vacant building that can be adapted as a chicken house – perhaps a disused calf shed or stable. This will certainly reduce the costs of setting up the enterprise. If the floor shows signs of damp then put in a new concrete floor with a plastic membrane; plug holes in brickwork and stonework and plaster walls flat with a mixture of sand and cement (or get someone to do this for you). Flat walls are much easier to keep clean and provide far fewer homes for bugs.

If the roof is of corrugated iron, line it with matchboard or chipboard and give the iron a good coat of metal preservative.

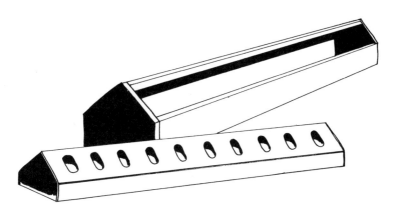

Feeders

Put in a south facing plastic window and any ventilation aids you think necessary like a wire mesh grille above the door. Make the house a pleasant place for the hens to spend time in. Hens will not take kindly to a damp stuffy, re-furbished pig sty with a low roof.

Some free-range flocks are housed in sheds which can be moved on skids or wheels. Even free-range hens often spend a lot of time in the area immediately around their house and the idea of mobility is to prevent a build-up of disease. You may be able to acquire a movable house second-hand at a farm sale but the help of a friendly neighbour with a tractor and trailer may be needed to get it home. So don't let your hens peck his cabbages.

Equipment for Feeding and Drinking
Manufacturers have not been slow in responding to the increasing interest in domestic poultry-keeping, and equipment for feeding and watering hens is readily available.

Hens kept in batteries live in a world of gadgetry – nipple drinkers for water, automatic feeders, artificial daylight and cages designed to make new-laid eggs roll away out of reach of bored hens. There is no need for the domestic poultryman to bother with such devices and some of the equipment can be home made. Feeders and drinkers are normally galvanized but plastic drinkers are also available and are often cheaper.

Food can be given in either troughs or self-feed hoppers, although some of the food for free-range hens can simply be scattered on the ground. Hoppers are containers for dry mash, corn, pellets or grit, and as the birds feed so more of the food slips down. Normally they are kept under cover either in the house itself or under a covered section of the run to keep the contents dry. Like drinkers they are best suspended on wire to stop rodents getting at the food but make sure they are not too high for the hens to use.

One of the advantages of using a hopper is that the hens can be left if you want to go away, as long as the reservoir of food is sufficient. If your hens are free-ranging though, you will still need the services of a friendly neighbour to open the house in the morning and lock it again at night.

The simplest form of open trough is a length of guttering screwed to timber blocks and long enough to accommodate the

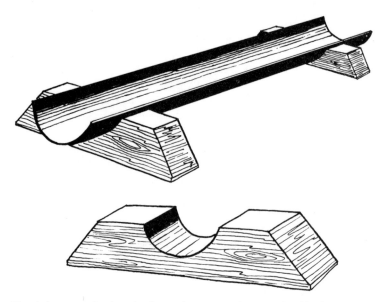

Simple hopper using length of guttering mounted on wooden blocks

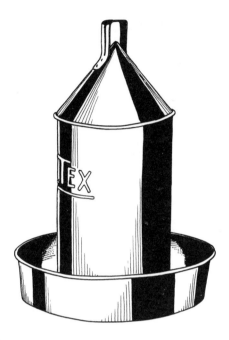

Chick Drinker

Simple Water Fount

hens. Allow 6 in of trough space for each one or the weaker birds may get crowded out. A V-shaped trough can be made by screwing two planks together. Lining the trough with aluminium or tin will help when it comes to cleaning but make sure there are no sharp edges to injure the birds – or yourself.

Drinkers can also be home-made, but proprietary drinkers of galvanized metal or plastic do not cost much and will last for years. The second-hand market at farm sales is worth exploring for suitable equipment. Sometimes poultry equipment goes for next to nothing – but give it a thorough cleaning before you start using it.

A do-it-yourself drinker can be made with an upturned plastic bottle secured to an L-shaped wooden frame. The correct gap between bottle and bowl can be worked out only through trial and error – if too wide all the water runs out. A car tyre cut in two and suspended from a low branch or even a timber tripod is a cheap and efficient drinker and can also be used as a feeder.

Scoops to measure out food can be made quite simply by cutting the bottom off a plastic bottle. You can get splendid brass scoops with wooden handles for the same purpose but most of them now seem to belong in antique shops. Cut-down plastic drink bottles are much cheaper.

Sectioned car tyre as simple water trough

3

ACQUIRING STOCK

All breeds of hens lay eggs but some are better at it than others. There are a number of options when considering what stock to acquire, but the choice really boils down to whether you want point-of-lay pullets or hens. A pullet is a bird which is either about to start laying or is already into its first laying year; a hen is into its second.

Another possibility is buying day-old chicks – beautiful fluffy things which will provide a daily fascination for the younger members of the family and, in all probability, their parents as well. Day-old chicks are much cheaper to buy than pullets or hens but you will have to face the cost of rearing them up to point-of-lay and financially things will work out about the same. Day-old chicks need warmth and a lot of attention for the first few weeks, and waiting perhaps twenty weeks for the arrival of the first egg may stretch the patience of the first-time poultryman anxious to get into production. Rearing your own can always be tried in later years and the first-timer is best advised to start with something older.

Pullets

Pullets sold as being at 'point-of-lay' are, in theory, precisely that – on the point of laying their first egg when they are sixteen to eighteen weeks old, or maybe slightly older. But do not expect to start getting eggs the day after you get them home. Moving the pullets from wherever they have been reared can delay the arrival of the first egg, as indeed can moving them from one shed to another a few feet away.

It might be better to buy the pullets when they are slightly younger, perhaps at around thirteen to fourteen weeks, which will give them time to settle into their new surroundings before they start laying – but find out exactly how old they are before buying.

Hens

Hens are cheaper than pullets but they will lay fewer eggs because they will have already been through their first laying season which is the period of maximum production.

If you are going to buy hens, as distinct from pullets, then take along someone who knows a bit about poultry. The points to watch out for in a laying hen are bright and alert eyes, bright red comb, firm and erect, and clean feathers around the vent area. Ruffled feathers around the vent area are said to indicate frequent trips to the nesting box and thus a good layer but that is open to some doubt. Whatever you buy make sure it has been vaccinated against fowl pest (Newcastle Disease). You should

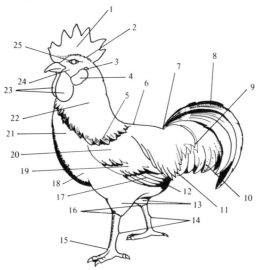

POINTS OF A FOWL

1	comb	10	tail coverts	18	point of heel – bone
2	base of comb	11	saddle hackle	19	wing coverts
3	ear	12	abdomen	20	wing – bow
4	ear lobe (large and fleshy)	13	thighs	21	breast
5	cape	14	spurs	22	neck hackle
6	back	15	shank or leg	23	wattles
7	saddle	16	hocks	24	face
8	sickles	17	primaries	25	eye
9	tail (main feathers)				

try to buy hens of the same colour too, and that is not as daft as it may sound. Having more white hens than brown may result in the brown ones being pecked and shouldered out at feeding time.

The basic reason for keeping hens is to produce your own fresh eggs – whether they are brown-shelled eggs, white or, in some cases, speckled. But there is another factor to be considered: Will the hens make decent table birds when they have been through two years of laying, and production is on the verge of dropping to an uneconomic level?

This business of killing may sound unpleasant but it is a fact which has to be faced eventually. There is little point in the small-scale poultryman keeping hens beyond their useful laying life – unless of course money is no object and the feed bill is not going to break the family budget. Unfortunately – for the hens that is – most people do not fall within that category.

Selection of Breed
What is needed when selecting a suitable breed is a bird that will lay a good supply of eggs and will also, when her economic laying days are over, provide the family with Sunday lunch – in other words a dual-purpose breed. The modern commercial hybrids on which the supermarkets depend have been bred from two or more breeds to lay lots of uniform-sized eggs over a comparatively short period. They have achieved their commercial dominance because of their efficiency at converting food into eggs – not meat – and as table birds they tend to be on the lean side. But there are a number of traditional dual-purpose breeds including the Rhode Island Red, the Light Sussex and others, which will perhaps be less well-known, like the Plymouth Rock and the Wyandotte. All four are among the 'heavy' breeds.

The 'light' breeds which are good layers but which have less merit as table birds include the Leghorns and the Anconas. The 'heavy' breeds are poor fliers and confining them to a run is easier than with the 'light' breeds.

All those mentioned so far are pure breeds (see list at end of chapter), which means they have the blood of only one breed in them. Tracking down a supplier of pure breeds might prove difficult, and one alternative is to go for a proven cross-bred like the Rhode Island Red crossed with a Light Sussex (RIR x LS).

The Rhode is a good layer, the best of the 'heavy' breeds, and the Sussex provides a meaty carcass. The Rhode is also often crossed with the White Leghorn, which is a champion laying breed. Another possible choice of cross-bred, the Arbor Acre, is a cross between the Rhode Island Red and the Barred Plymouth Rock.

Countless smallholders and back garden poultrymen have started out with crosses of Rhode with Light Sussex or the Rhode with White Leghorn because both have established records. But hybrids should not be ruled out completely. Although bred for intensive commercial conditions many hybrids perform very well as free-range birds or in back garden units. The one problem with hybrids is that broodiness – the maternal instinct of a hen wanting to sit on a clutch of eggs – has largely been bred out because commercially a broody hen is a non-productive hen. Hens do not lay while they are broody.

This is not always the case, though, and some hybrids do go broody and make fine mothers, but generally a cross-bred or a pure-bred is much more likely to go broody than a hybrid. So if at some future stage you plan to let a broody hatch out a clutch of fertile eggs and rear up the chicks then a cross-bred is a better bet.

Buying Pullets

Where do you get the pullets from? The importance of buying from a reputable breeder cannot be overstressed. It is possible to buy pullets at markets, even those in large towns, but unless you are accompanied by a poultry keeper of some experience you will not know either what you are buying or what to look out for. There are plenty of pitfalls in buying 'bargain basement' pullets. The so-called pullets may in fact be two- or three-year-old hens which are well past their best. They may sound cheap, but buying them is false economy.

Go to a reputable breeder instead. Checking the advertisements in the local paper or Yellow Pages should reveal a source. A large breeder might not want to be bothered with an order for half a dozen pullets but he should be able to suggest someone who will be. You may also have made contact with other domestic poultrymen and they should know where to go for good stock.

Try to buy pullets that are due to come into lay around August or September. With the right feeding, and possibly the use of supplementary lighting in the house during winter to compensate for the shortened daylight, the pullets will lay for the following twelve months before undergoing their first moult when they will shed some of their feathers and cease laying for a while.

This means a period of no eggs unless an earlier surplus has been preserved in the freezer or by some other method. When the moult is over the hens will start laying again and will continue until the next moult in September or October and that is the moment of decision. Do you keep the hens on, despite the fact that egg production is declining from previously high levels, or do you wring their necks and put them in the freezer?

In a properly managed domestic unit this is also when replacement pullets either bought in at point-of-lay or reared up from day-old should just be starting to lay. Without doubt clearing out hens every two years makes a lot of economic sense for the domestic poultryman just as it does for the battery owner, only *he* does not wait that long.

Discarded Battery Stock

Another possible source of stock is to buy the birds that have been discarded by the battery houses after one or two years. Most ex-battery birds are slaughtered and end up in soups, stock cubes, meat pastes and the like but sometimes they can be bought for as little as fifty pence apiece. The appearance of some of these birds might, however, be somewhat distressing. They may, for example, be almost totally denuded of feathers and have difficulty in walking, which is not too surprising after months in a wire cage.

Once released from their life behind bars, though, battery birds often readily adapt to a changed environment and soon learn to scratch, take dust baths and to lay eggs in dark secluded corners and in comfy boxes rather than in wire cages in full view of hundreds of other birds. Ex-battery birds might have trouble at first using both nest boxes and perches. They may require to be gently lifted onto the perches at night but pretty soon they will get the hang of life outside the battery.

Battery birds will continue to lay reasonable numbers of eggs

Rhode Island Red

for three or four years, or even longer, but their period of top production is over, so if costs are the prime consideration perhaps it is better not to bother with them. If, on the other hand, you want to provide a good home for a few refugees and get some eggs into the bargain, then go ahead. The hens will be most grateful. Surprisingly ex-battery birds often make very good free-rangers.

THE PURE-BREEDS INCLUDE

Heavy Breeds

Rhode Island Red: A North American breed (from Rhode Island, U.S.A.), the Rhode was imported at the turn of the century and is one of the most easily managed of all breeds. A good breed for both meat and eggs, the Rhode, with its rich red colour and deep broad shoulders, is often described as being like a 'housebrick with the corners knocked off' which hardly does it justice. Adult males weight up to $8\frac{1}{2}$ lb and females 5 to $6\frac{1}{2}$ lb. The Rhode does well on free-range and the hens make excellent mothers.

Wyandottes: Like the White Sussex the Wyandotte, which is also of American origin, is a good winter layer. There are thirteen varieties but the White is among the most popular and one of the best layers. Other varieties include Gold Laced, Silver Laced, Gold Pencilled and Silver Pencilled. A dual-purpose breed, the cocks weigh between 7 and 8 lb and the hens between 5 and 7 lb.

Sussex Fowl: These come in a number of different colours including Light, Red, Speckled and Brown but the Light Sussex is the most popular. The Light Sussex is white-feathered apart from a black neck and tail. Sussex are large-bodied birds and make good table fowl but do not lay as well as the Rhode. Full grown cocks weigh between 8 and 10 lb.

Light Breeds

Leghorns: Originally from North West Italy, Leghorns have been bred in a dozen different colours but White, Black and

Brown are the most familiar, especially the White. Irrespective of colour their eggs are the same – white-shelled. The Leghorn adapts well to the confines of a restricted unit and, bearing in mind its prolific egg-laying capacity, eats a smaller quantity of food than some other breeds.

Ancona: Another of the Mediterranean breeds (Leghorn, Minorca, Andalusian) all classified as light, Anconas were first introduced into the U.K. in the 1850s and are prolific layers of white eggs. But they are regarded as rather flighty birds and require good fencing to keep them in. The Ancona has green-black plumage with white tips and yellow legs mottled with black. Like the Leghorn they do not go broody easily and do not make good table birds. Kept free-range though they are good foragers.

White Leghorn

Minorca: The largest of the Mediterranean breeds — both male and female can weigh up to 8 lb — the Minorca has a good reputation as a layer of large white eggs but is a lean table bird. Despite being hardy and adaptable the popularity of the breed has declined.

Bantams: As an alternative to all these breeds Bantams are another possibility. They are small-scale birds that eat less, and there are Bantam versions of most varieties of full-size poultry including Rhode Island, Sussex, Plymouth Rock, Wyandotte, although others are distinct breeds in their own right. Some poultry enthusiasts keep nothing but Bantams. Because of their size their housing requirements are less, and they eat less too, but they average fewer eggs a year — about 100 — and these are smaller so the cost equation works out at about the same. Bantams are full of character — much more than their full-size brethren — and have a jerky walk. But some varieties are difficult to keep in restricted wire runs because they are masters of the art of escaping and if kept free-range they have a tendency to lay in their own nests rather than in those provided in the hen house. But, when broody, Bantams generally make very good mothers, although because of their size cannot look after as many chicks as full-size broodies.

4

FEEDING

The hen's digestive system consists of the crop, which is where food first passes after being swallowed, the stomach, the gizzard and intestines.

The crop at the base of the throat is a bag in the food pipe which bulges noticeably after feeding. It is in the crop that the first stage of the food softening process takes place by the action of saliva.

The gizzard is a dark red organ with strong muscular walls which acts in a similar way to the stomach churning the food up into a mush ready for the action of the intestines.

Insoluble grit – flint or granite – is retained in the gizzard and, aided by the muscular action of the gizzard walls, helps to grind the food up. This grinding process will take place without any grit being present but not so effectively which means that the hen is not making the fullest use of the food eaten.

When free-range a hen will find some of her own grit – both insoluble grit for the gizzard and soluble limestone for the calcium required in forming the egg shell. But in the restricted system of the back garden run, both will have to be supplied, as indeed will all the other key ingredients of the hen's diet.

The waste products of the hen and the eggs are produced through the same vent. The ova, or egg yolk, is made in the ovary and slides into the oviduct which is a long tube ending at the vent. In the first part of the oviduct the albumen – the egg white – is formed around the yolk, and in the second part the shell is formed. The whole egg-making process takes about twenty hours although there may be two or three eggs in the oviduct at different stages of production. The egg is laid blunt end first and is already hard when laid. It does not, as many people think, harden up after being laid.

Good feeding is vital and is the biggest recurring expense in keeping poultry. Commercially the food bill represents about 70 per cent of total production costs. Correct feeding means the difference between a healthy and a sickly hen; the difference between a good layer and a poor layer; the difference between profit and loss.

The cheapest possible diet of wheat, household scraps and water will result in some eggs, but a diet with the right amount of protein, vitamins and minerals will produce far more. People do not function well on junk food and the same applies to hens so do not be misled into thinking that hens in a back garden run are going to survive and lay well on a make-do diet of kitchen left-overs. Neither, for that matter, will the free-range hen, although she should be able to get up to half her daily food requirements from her own foraging.

Feed can be supplemented with domestic waste and produce from the garden, but both these should be regarded as additions rather than substitutes. At the most, household left-overs and garden produce should account for only about one-fifth of the ration of a healthy laying hen.

A Balanced Diet

To lay well and to keep in prime condition a hen needs a balanced diet containing at least 15 per cent protein, plus fats, carbohydrates, vitamins and some minerals. The easiest, although unfortunately not the cheapest, way to provide this is to buy in pre-mixed layers' food in 55 lb sacks from corn merchants or agricultural suppliers. Pet shops sometimes stock it but in smaller quantities and it is normally more expensive. Check in Yellow Pages for the nearest animal feedstuff supplier.

This bagged food comes either pelletized ('layers' pellets') or in the form of a dry powder ('layers' mash') which can be fed either wet or dry. Pellets, which are always fed dry, are quicker and easier to use than mash, although they may cost slightly more. Using pellets the birds can help themselves from a self-service hopper, an idea which might suit the poultryman who has only limited time. If the hens *are* fed on a hopper they may gorge themselves for the first few days before settling down to eat as much as they need.

It is difficult to be precise about how much each hen will

require a day because this depends on the age and type of bird, the rate of laying and even the weather. If the birds are being hand-fed twice a day, then give them what they will clear up in ten minutes. If any food is left over you are over-feeding and, because hens prefer their food to be as fresh as possible, left-over food is often wasted. Over-feeding can be dangerous too. It does not lead to more eggs; it simply leads to a fat, unhealthy layer. As a general guide feed each hen $2\frac{1}{2}$-3 oz a day of a balanced diet – pellets or mash – but increase this slightly in cold weather.

It may be possible to cut feeding costs and still maintain a healthy diet by substituting some of the balanced food with mixed corn, which is a mixture of wheat, barley, oats and maize. You could try feeding a couple of ounces of wet mash to each hen in the morning and two ounces of mixed corn in the afternoon. Mixed corn is normally cheaper than either mash or pellets and is available from the same source.

Wheat by itself has a protein content of about 10 per cent and is a good feed for laying hens when mixed with something else like pellets. Barley has a protein content of about 6 per cent, but by itself hens soon seem to get tired of it. Try mixing it with wheat. Layers' mash can be fed either wet or dry. Feeding dry can lead to some of the food being wasted and since bought-in foods are expensive the less wasted the better.

Wetting the mash with water until it is moist and crumbly in the fingers – not sloppy like a brown soup – reduces waste but the mixing does take time, a commodity which may be in short supply for the suburban poultryman who has to commute to work each morning. One solution might be to feed dry mash in the morning and wet mash at night with boiled household scraps added.

Vegetable Matter

This diet can be supplemented with a variety of food from the garden, so when planting out the vegetable plot put in some extra for the hens. The cost of doing so is negligible. Although green food contains little egg-producing material it does have some vitamins and helps to give the yolks a deep richer colour.

Maize helps in that respect too and so do carrots. Any of the brassicas can be fed but it is largely a waste of time throwing a bunch of cabbage leaves into the run because if they get dirty the hens won't touch them. Instead tie the bunch to a post or the wire of the run with a slip knot so that when the hens jump up and pull on the leaves the knot tightens.

Hanging the leaves out of normal reach compels the birds to jump and the exercise helps to keep them fit and healthy. It also reduces the risk of boredom setting in. Feather pecking, as mentioned earlier, is a sign of boredom, and bored, unhappy hens make bad layers. Alternatively, instead of hanging the leaves up, chop them finely and pop them in a string bag inside the run and let the birds peck. Greenstuff should be fed regularly and throughout the year, not just in the summer when supplies will be plentiful from the garden.

Lettuce, cabbage, cauliflower, broccoli, sprout leaves and sprouts, should you be lucky enough to have a surplus of those, can all be fed. Parsnips, carrots, turnips and swedes can be finely chopped and fed by themselves or, if the hens are on a wet mash diet, mixed in with that. Leaves of comfrey can be hung up for the birds to peck at too. Chives can also be mixed in with the mash, and marrow skins can be boiled and fed with mash or other scraps. Certain garden weeds are also useful for feeding, including the appropriately named chickweed and fat hen. Fat hen, of which tons are dug up and thrown away by gardeners each year, is high in iron, vitamin B and calcium and has a higher protein level than cabbage.

Lawn clippings can be used as a green food, but make certain that they have not been sprayed with weed killers. Other food possibilities are mountain ash berries, beech nuts, sweet chestnut, horse chestnut, crushed home-grown sunflower seeds and dried and crushed acorns. Avoid rhubarb and the sprouts of potatoes – both of which are harmful to hens.

Kitchen Waste

Kitchen waste which can be used includes any stale bread, potatoes, potato peelings, pudding and cake waste, and scraps of meat and fish. All of these must be cooked first for easy digestion and to reduce the possibility of disease. Fish bones can be rendered down in a pressure cooker and fed as part of a mash meal. Do not expect your hens to eat anything that has started decomposing.

Scrapings from meal plates are best avoided because hens

cannot tolerate salt, and too much fat, a common ingredient in household scraps, may cause the hens to put on excess weight and to stop laying.

Calcium

The other essentials of good diet, apart from clean and fresh water, are calcium for egg shell formation and insoluble grit for retention in the gizzard. Calcium is given in the form of crushed oyster or ground limestone – both obtainable at corn merchants or pet shops or by crushing up the shells of the hen's own eggs. The simplest way of doing this is to bake the shells in a slow oven and then crush them with a rolling pin.

Insoluble grit for the gizzard is either flint or granite grit. Separate containers of both grit and crushed shell can be provided under cover for the hens or the two can be mixed in the ratio of one part insoluble grit to four parts crushed oyster shell or egg shell and fed once a week allowing $\frac{1}{2}$ oz for each bird.

Feeding is best carried out when the house is opened in the morning and again in the later afternoon about one hour before dusk – unless of course hoppers are being used which means you are not tied to set feeding times.

Feed Storage

A cheap storage container for grain or pellets is a metal dustbin which will be big enough to hold several weeks supply of food for half a dozen hens. Keep the dustbin in the garage or porch or anywhere out of the rain and make sure the lid is a good tight fit to foil rodents. Another possibility is using a milk churn. The lids of churns are very close fitting and a 10 gallon churn easily holds 55 lb of food.

There is not much point in bulk-buying food with only half a dozen or a dozen hens because it may have gone stale by the time it is needed. The hens will not enjoy it and neither will it do them much good, so any cost benefits will be lost. For the smallholder with a larger flock, though, bulk-buying of wheat, mixed corn and pellets should be cheaper. The storage of large quantities will require a purpose-built bin normally made of metal with a hinged lid. They can sometimes be picked up cheaply at farm auctions or you could try making your own to hold a ton or half a ton, using timber and lining the interior with zinc, aluminium or even second-hand corrugated iron sheets to deter rats.

It may also be possible if you have the space available in an outbuilding to make a permanent storage bin from four inch concrete blocks. Whatever you decide make sure that the storage bin will keep the contents dry and be rodent-proof.

Winter Egg Supplies

Daylight is a key factor in egg production. Left to her own devices a hen lays more eggs in the spring and summer than during the winter when the hours of daylight are less. The hen is stimulated into laying by light falling on the retina of the eye. This causes the pituitary gland to produce a secretion which in turn stimulates activity affecting the ovaries.

Less light means fewer eggs and winter, especially during the dark days of December when daylight is down to seven hours, is the worst time for egg production. Even a pullet which came into lay the previous July or August will lay fewer eggs.

The solution is to borrow a technique from the battery and lengthen the hours of daylight artificially with electric lighting. Increasing the natural winter production does not, however, mean that the hen will lay more eggs over the whole twelve months but simply evens out her monthly production. You may not want to interfere with the hen in this way preferring instead to let her lay more in the summer and preserving the surplus eggs in water-glass or in the freezer for the winter.

If, on the other hand, you want to maintain egg production in winter, artificial lighting is needed to give the hens fifteen hours of light each day. If natural daylight is down to eight hours this means extra lighting in the chicken house for another seven. Normally this is done using a light for a period in the morning and again in the evening. For a shed measuring 6 ft x 4 ft a 25 watt bulb is adequate, and wiring this into a time clock will cut out the need to switch it on and off in the morning and again at night. Get a qualified electrician to do the wiring for you if you are uncertain how to do it yourself. As the days lengthen in January and February less artificial light is required and the timer will need re-setting weekly until natural daylight has increased to fifteen hours again.

Winter Housing

Hens do not like rain, snow or mud, and in bad winter weather are better off confined to a house rather than hanging around outdoors in a muddy run. If the run is covered, of course, confinement is not necessary. If they have to be confined make sure they have enough room (a 6 ft x 4 ft properly ventilated house is large enough for six birds for a short while) and enough food. Hens require slightly more food in winter so make sure they get it along with plenty of greenstuff, grit and a dust bath in a box. Change the drinking water regularly and make sure it remains unfrozen in frosty weather. Ensure also that the floor of the house is dry and covered with a good layer of litter like peat moss, chopped straw or wood shavings to keep it warm. Greenstuff can be hung up in the house to give the hens some exercise, although on fine days they can be allowed out into the run.

Some free-range flocks are brought indoors during winter, and egg production is maintained with artificial lighting; other free-range birds are left to wander around outside in the hope that they will continue to lay in useful numbers. A possible compromise is to confine the hens during bad weather in a house with artificial lighting, but giving them access to an adjoining open scratching and exercise area during the day when they can get the benefit of any sunny spells.

Adequate ventilation is essential during periods of confinement as is floor litter. The outside exercise area can also be littered with well chopped straw and will require fencing to stop the hens flying out. Allow about 3 sq ft of space for each bird in the house, although the scratching area can be smaller. Nest boxes, feeders and drinkers remain in the house but some of the food can be fed in the exercise area when the weather is suitable to encourage the birds to scratch and exercise among the straw. When the weather has improved sufficiently the hens can go back to free-ranging.

5

DISEASES

Prevention is better than cure. Buying sound, healthy stock, providing the right housing, feeding correctly and keeping both house and run clean will go a long way towards avoiding illness and disease in your chicken flock. Kept properly hens are healthy and hardy creatures but, even in the best managed unit, troubles can break out so it is as well to know how to recognize ailments and what to do about them.

There are some definite 'don'ts'. Don't panic because one of your hens looks decidedly off-colour; don't rush off to the nearest library to read up on poultry diseases; don't call out the vet on the vague suspicion that the entire flock is suffering from some creeping killer disease. Panicking will do no one any good and your own health least of all; boning up on diseases from library books will convince you that all your hens are suffering from every disease known to veterinary science and will all be dead within hours; calling out the vet to have a look at one poorly hen is expensive.

If you have a smallholding and the vet is coming out anyway on a routine visit to check other livestock then ask him to take a look at the suspect hen while he is with you. But calling him out to have a look at one suspect chicken is an expensive way of sorting out the trouble. His call-out fee plus whatever drugs or medicines he supplies will in all probability be more than the poor old hen is worth.

If you really want an expert opinion then take the bird to the vet yourself thereby avoiding his call-out fee. Some, but by no means all, vets will bring the same skill, care and attention to a hen worth a few pounds that they will give to a pedigree cow worth thousands. But you are far more likely to find a ministering angel such as this in a rural rather than a suburban practice.

Warning Signs

Watch your hens regularly and be on the look-out for any change in habits. One of the advantages of hand feeding over self-feed hoppers is that it gives an opportunity for a good look at the birds twice a day when any signs of trouble can be spotted early on. If, for example, a hen is crouched down totally disinterested while the rest are eating, then that is a sure sign that something is wrong.

The state of the droppings is also a good tell-tale sign as to the condition of the hen. The droppings should be firmly formed, dark brown or black and topped with white. Droppings that are loose, watery and greenish are an indication that all is not well. The trouble, however, may be no more serious than dietary. Hens do sometimes go off their food, especially if it has been allowed to go stale in the trough through overfeeding and putting fresh food on top of food left over from a previous meal. If food is being left in the troughs then clear it away before adding fresh – and cut down on the ration. Food is too expensive to waste.

Diarrhoea can be caused by feeding too much of any one grain, such as maize, or excessive soluble grit or by a hen drinking water that has been warmed by the sun so make sure that drinkers are kept in the shade. The trouble may clear itself up but, if not, then isolate the affected hen in a coop, change her diet and see if she recovers. If the trouble is contagious it will quickly show up among the other birds.

Worms and Parasites

Hens are susceptible to disease picked up off the ground and internal parasites can be spread through droppings. Changing the location of a back garden run if a movable unit is being used, or switching the hens from one permanent run to another will help to prevent a build-up of worms and parasites which, if unchecked, can quickly reduce healthy hens to sickly, unproductive wrecks. A small, overcrowded run on the same site provides the ideal conditions for a build-up of parasites. The idea of using fresh ground regularly prevents one patch getting stale, tired and 'chicken sick'.

Lime which is available in plastic bags from agricultural merchants or garden shops can be spread over used runs to help rot down the droppings and the earth can be forked over. Care is needed when using lime. Hydrated lime can cause chemical burns and common-sense protective clothing should be worn. If in doubt contact I.C.I.'s Public Relations Office at Millbank, London SW1 3JF or read the H.M.S.O. booklet on lime and liming.

Remember that each hen produces roughly one hundredweight of droppings a year and, since about half that will be deposited outside, then a regular change of run is essential. For hens that are free-ranging the risk of picking up diseases from the ground is much less of a problem but they too should be watched closely for signs of trouble.

COMMON PROBLEMS

These are some of the problems you may have to face:

Egg Eating

This is neither a disease nor an illness – it is simply a nuisance. It starts when a hen either lays an egg while roosting which breaks on hitting the ground (since eggs and waste products come out of the same hole mistakes can happen) or she lays an egg without a shell. Other inquisitive hens then quickly discover the tastiness of eggs and the trouble can transfer itself to the nest boxes with some hens breaking open their own freshly-laid eggs or the eggs of other hens. This means dirty nest boxes and a drop in profitability.

Egg eating is often the result of overcrowding and boredom for hens kept in a run. The remedy for overcrowding is obvious – get rid of some of the hens or put them in a larger run. Boredom can be solved by keeping the birds interested and active by giving them greenstuff to jump at. Egg eating may also be a sign that the nest boxes are too light so make sure they do not face a window, and darken the front of the box if necessary with strips of sacking or thin carpet over the front.

You can try filling an eggshell with mustard to deter egg eating but in my experience this is not a guaranteed way of beating the problem. Some hens seem to like the taste of mustard too. Soft shelled eggs are not unusual in a bird just starting to lay and they will harden up after a short time. Soft shelled eggs in older layers, however, indicate a lack of calcium or green food.

Feather Pecking

This is another nuisance, but with potentially far more serious results, and is far more likely to occur in confined runs rather than on free range. Idleness is one possible cause along with overcrowding and poor diet.

The back, rump and tail are commonly affected regions and in some cases one hen can completely remove a feather from another leading to the possibility of cannibalism breaking out with fatal results.

A hen which has been feather pecked should be taken out and isolated in a coop. The trouble is difficult to stop once it has started but increasing the food ration and hanging up extra greenstuff so that the birds have less idle time should help. Proprietary anti-pecking sprays are also available. If a hen is suffering from broken skin as a result of being pecked the affected area should be treated with Stockholm Tar, a substance which looks like thick black paint, available from chemists and some vets. This discourages further attacks and helps the wound to heal.

If all attempts to solve the feather pecking problem fail, then the only answer may be for a vet to trim the bird's beak using a trimmer with electrically heated blades which removes and cauterizes a portion of the beak. This, however, should be regarded as a last resort. In a well-managed domestic flock, where there is no overcrowding and sufficient food and water are being provided, feather pecking is unlikely to be a problem.

Crop-Bound

Chickens — and geese and ducks — sometimes have difficulty eating because bits of long grass, straw or hay have clogged the crop making it swollen. The simplest cure is to give the hen a teaspoonful of warm water — or administer it with a plastic syringe — and gently rub the crop. By holding the bird with its head down the crop can be pressed gently and the obstruction squeezed out. Then let the hen drink freely and isolate it without food for a day.

Laying Disorders

Birds in their first year's lay have few laying problems. The first eggs may look narrow in shape and in some cases the shells may carry streaks of blood but there is no need for alarm. When a pullet first comes into lay the oviduct is narrow and the first few eggs can cause the bird some difficulty. The narrow passage results in the slightly elongated shape and the blood streaks are caused by the rupture of small blood vessels.

In some cases a pullet may be unable to pass an egg because the oviduct is too small. This is known as egg binding and one solution is to soften the pelvic bones by holding the bird with her vent exposed to steam from hot water. Common-sense − on which so much of poultrykeeping is based − will tell you how far the bird should be held from the steam source and how hot the steam should be.

Laying troubles can become a problem in the second year lay and occasionally a portion of the oviduct can protrude, either through straining or the laying of over-sized eggs. This is called a prolapse and affected birds should be isolated as soon as the trouble is detected because healthy hens can be vicious to a sickly colleague.

Wash the area with tepid water, smear the protrusion with lubricating jelly and very gently push it back with the finger. Keep the affected hen warm for a few days and halve her normal diet. The protrusion may reappear and the exercise may have to be repeated a few times. But if the treatment fails then the only solution is to kill the bird.

Coccidiosis

Chickens can be infected by many different species of coccidia − parasites which live in the cells lining the gut and eventually destroy them. Infectious cysts are passed out in the droppings and the parasite can build up quickly in a badly managed run. Affected birds produce a watery diarrhoea which may be bloodstained. Drugs obtainable from vets can be put into the drinking water to kill off the disease but if the run is moved or changed regularly, and used areas allowed to rest for as long as possible, coccidiosis is unlikely to be a problem in the first place.

Fowl Pest

Also known as Newcastle Disease, this can be the big killer among commercial flocks, but outbreaks among small numbers of domestic birds are rare. However, it is a sensible precaution when buying stock to make sure it has been vaccinated against the disease. The symptoms include sneezing, gasping, a drop in egg yield, listlessness, green diarrhoea and misshapen or soft-shelled eggs. Fowl Pest is a notifiable disease which means that if suspected it must be reported to the Police, the Ministry of Agriculture or a vet. The dead bodies should be buried in quicklime.

Avian Tuberculosis

Avian tuberculosis, which is not notifiable, produces abscesses in the liver, spleen and lungs and the symptoms include loss of appetite and lameness. There is no cure and if several birds in the flock are affected then the rest may have to be culled too. As with Fowl Pest the bodies should be buried in quicklime. Diagnosis is best left to the vet.

Mites and Lice

Regular cleaning and disinfecting of the hen house, changing nest box straw and creosoting perches will go a long way towards avoiding problems caused by lice and mites. Pay special attention to perch sockets and dark corners where mites live during the day. If the hen house is an old stone building the walls are best plastered to avoid providing cosy crevices for mites.

One of the worst of these parasites is the *red mite*, a blood sucker which looks like a miniature spider and attacks at night. When filled with blood it takes on a bright red colour although this changes to a pale grey as the blood is digested. Newly-hatched eggs from female mites can become active blood suckers themselves after twenty-four hours and a heavy infestation can build up rapidly leading to anaemic hens and a drop in eggs. One way to check whether red mites are present is to examine the house and the birds at night with the aid of a torch.

Treatment is best carried out by spraying the house with an insecticide like pyrethrum or malathion – although there are others – and by removing and burning litter. Lice live on the feathers or the skin and because of their clawed legs the hen is unable to shake them off by normal preening or by scratching with her feet. One kind of lice prefers the feathers on the neck and top of the head and another, known as the broad body louse, likes the fluffy small feathers around the vent area.

Apart from spoiling the appearance of the birds the presence of lice causes irritation and restlessness which may lead to a drop in egg production. The *hen flea* is the only species of flea that attacks poultry in the U.K. and feeds on roosting birds before going off to hide in any dark corners of the house or even in nesting boxes.

Dusting each bird with a proprietary louse powder – available from vets and some chemists – will keep the trouble under control. The powder should be rubbed well into the feathers, under the wings and between the legs. A build-up of crusty deposits under the scales of the feet and legs indicates *scaly leg mite*. This mite burrows into the skin restricting a bird's ability to perch comfortably or hunt for food. Badly affected birds may end up with deformed feet and possibly the loss of several toes. The chalky crusts can be removed after first softening with warm, soapy water and then painting the legs with benzyl benzoate obtainable from vets.

Dust Baths

Humans like baths and so do hens and the only difference is that hens do it in dust. A regular dust bath goes a long way towards eradicating problems caused by parasites. The simplest way to make a dust bath is to scoop out a depression in the run and fill it with earth or sand or both and let the hens wallow in it. They will flick the soil and sand over themselves and between their feathers and then shake it all out. Dust baths also help the birds to keep cool in hot weather. If you do not want a cratered back garden use a wooden box instead and, if you like, add a sprinkling of louse powder to the dust too.

Free-range hens will find their own dust baths in all manner of places. Any old pile of building sand will quickly be taken over and turned into a communal bathroom.

Two final tips on beating the illness problem: louse powder sprinkled on the nest straw will help to prevent parasites, and a clove of garlic finely cut up and added to a gallon of drinking water helps to keep the hens free of intestinal worms. Some poultrymen swear by the use of garlic.

Handling Poultry

Good management includes a regular examination of the birds for lice and any injuries that might need treatment. The easiest time to pick up and check over the birds is when they have

Correct method of picking up a bird

settled down on their perches for the night. The frequency of checking should not be overdone though. Hens do not like having their privacy invaded too often, and undue disturbance may cause them to go off lay. And do not, on any account, burst into the shed waving a stick. Remember − it is hens you are dealing with, not a herd of unco-operative cows.

With the bird facing you, pick her up with both hands, slide the hands under the breast gripping each thigh between two fingers. Then tuck the bird beneath one arm pressing the wings gently between elbow and body, with the bird's head pointing backwards. Your other hand is then free to check the feathers for lice and anything else that should not be there. You will need someone else standing by with a torch and, if necessary, the dusting powder.

While you have got the bird in your clutches this is a good time to carry out a rule-of-thumb test to see if she is in lay or not. The bird's pelvic bones, which are an inch or two above the top of the legs, are closer together when she is not in lay than when she is. If you can get three fingers between the bones the hen is almost certainly in lay; two fingers mean maybe; one suggests she is not. This is not an infallible guarantee though. Human fingers are not made in uniform sizes and neither are the pelvic bones of hens.

Moulting

This is a problem which you will definitely have to face. A pullet which starts laying in August or September will, with good feeding and management, lay for twelve months, maybe slightly longer, before losing her old feathers and growing fresh ones. This is known as moulting and will thereafter be an annual event for the rest of the bird's life. The start of the moult is fairly obvious because the hens will begin shedding their feathers and running around half-naked. The whole process of losing old feathers and replacing with new can take anything from six to twelve weeks, and during this time the hens will stop laying altogether.

The problem lies in getting the birds back into lay before the cold weather starts. Reducing the amount of food helps to achieve a quick 'feather drop' or even feeding a poorer quality food like wheat or mixed corn. As soon as the new feathers start appearing, switch back to higher protein pellets or mash or whatever system you use and greenstuffs to build the bird up again into lay.

6

REARING

However healthy and active your hens may be they are not, unfortunately, going to remain in peak production for long. The first year's lay will see the best performance, and production in the second will be down by around 25 per cent. After that it will drop further. Feed costs, though, will tend to rise so what do you do — kill them after two years for the freezer (and eventually the casserole) or keep them on the staff and accept a lower return?

Killing is dealt with in the next chapter but long before you get to the moment of decision (or indecision) some thought will have to be given about acquiring replacement stock which will be ready to come into lay just when your original birds are on their way out.

One way of acquiring replacements is simply to buy in fresh point-of-lay pullets. That is the easiest way but not the most interesting, especially if there are children in the household. The alternative to buying in fresh pullets is to rear up some chicks from one day old.

Where do you get the chicks from? In the natural world of a free-range flock of hens running with a cockerel the sex drive of the cock and the patience of a broody hen prepared to sit on a clutch of (hopefully) fertile eggs will solve the problem for you.

Even if you don't have a cockerel, a broody hen can still do most of the work for you by fostering day-old chicks bought from a breeder — perhaps the same breeder who supplied your original pullets.

Broodiness

A broody is the name given to a hen which has stopped laying for a while in order to hatch out eggs herself. This natural maternal instinct has been largely bred out of most hybrids since the aim of the commercial batteries is for egg-laying machines. Broodiness is simply not economical. Some hybrids never go broody and this is another factor to be considered when choosing the breed for the original flock.

The first sign of a broody hen is that she will stay on the nest for hours, often sitting on nothing at all. Any bird still sitting on the nest by the late afternoon and early evening is likely to be broody. When approached she will ruffle up her feathers and may even try to peck you and will make a sound like a low-pitched warning note which will be quite unlike any other hen sound.

The problem with using a broody hen to foster bought-in day-olds is that she is unlikely to be broody at the right time. What you should be aiming for are pullet chicks hatched in February or March which should be coming into lay when the older birds have either ceased laying temporarily because of the moult and the onset of colder weather, or have been despatched to the freezer. But broodiness may not take place until May or even later, which will mean a period of no eggs in the autumn because the older birds may not be laying and that year's pullets are too young.

One way out of this is to buy in day-olds and rear them yourself artificially which means you get exactly what you want and at the right time. Incubating your own eggs either artificially in an incubator or beneath a broody hen may result in half the new arrivals being cockerels and that is not much use if your principal aim is eggs rather than meat for the table. If the time you are able to devote to the poultry enterprise is limited, then raising a separate pen of growing cockerels will certainly mean extra work, and the crowing of young males at daybreak or even earlier might result in a rapid loss of patience amongst previously friendly neighbours.

Warmth, constant care and the right food are the essentials in raising chicks. There are a number of foster-mother devices, called brooders, for artificial rearing and basically they consist of a chamber, heated either by an oil lamp or electric element, in which the chicks sleep and an adjoining covered run for feeding and scratching. They are expensive items although it might be possible, as with much of all poultry equipment, to get one second-hand at a farm auction. If you can't buy, beg or borrow one, then make your own. Chicks can be successfully reared in nothing more sophisticated than a large cardboard or wooden box filled with hay and an infra-red lamp (see page 112 in the chapter on geese) or in a box in a warm airing cupboard. To drive out any damp (which can be fatal) the brooder will need to be warmed up for a day or two before the chicks are introduced. Heat the brooder up to around 90°F/32°C and keep it at that level for their first week of occupation. If you are using a 'hay box' and an infra-red bulb make sure the bulb hangs well above the chicks, because a burn could be fatal.

During the second week gradually lower the temperature to 85°F/30°C during the third to 80°F/27°C. For the following three weeks it should be around 70°F/21°C. Apart from using a thermometer the behaviour of the chicks will indicate whether the brooder is too hot or too cold. If it is too low they will 'cheep' plaintively and crowd around the heat source in a commercially made brooder; if too hot they will try to get as far away as possible and may gasp for breath.

Feeding Chicks

Correct feeding is as important as the right amount of heat, although for the first twenty-four hours they will not require feeding at all. After that give them a proprietary brand of chick crumbs or finely chopped hard-boiled egg mixed with breadcrumbs – wholemeal bread if you have got it. Proprietary chick crumbs – called 'starter crumbs' – are the easiest, though, because they have all the necessary ingredients for good diet and also contain an additive to prevent coccidiosis.

A tobacco tin makes a good feeder for half a dozen chicks, and little and often (say once every four hours during the daytime) is better than feeding large amounts. A broody hen teaches her chicks how to peck and they are quick learners, but in an artificial brooder they will not have much idea, so tapping their food tray with your fingers will help by exciting their curiosity. Chick crumbs are more easily digested if fed slightly damp, and a drop of cod liver oil can also be mixed in.

If using a commercially-made brooder the floor of the adjoining run can be littered with chopped straw and a handful of dry chick crumbs scattered in the run will encourage the chicks to peck, scratch and generally keep active. Fresh water in a shallow container is just as important as the feed, but make sure the container is not too deep or the chicks may drown. For a small number of chicks try a tobacco tin with a stone in the middle to stop them tipping it over.

At about six to eight weeks the chicks will have feathered up and 'hardened off', and can be transferred to an outside, unheated run. Common sense will tell you when this can be done. Obviously they should not be put outside during a sudden cold snap or a spell of monsoon-like weather. The run can be a small version of the fold unit mentioned earlier, or simply a waterproof box with a wire run attached. For half a dozen or a dozen chicks the run should be about 6 ft long, 2 ft wide and 2 ft high.

The chick starter crumbs can be continued for the first six weeks when the diet can be changed to grower's crumbs. Finely-ground baked egg shell can also be provided, and another useful addition to the feed is chickweed. Grower's crumbs can be continued up to sixteen weeks and then changed to a laying ration, either pellets or mash, with mixed corn occasionally.

A lawn or an orchard is excellent for rearing chicks and, if possible, use ground that has not been grazed by other poultry for at least six months to reduce the risk of the young stock picking up disease. Fresh water and greenstuff are essential during the rearing and the run will need to be moved regularly to clean ground. Make sure that the pullets have adequate shade in hot weather.

Incubating Eggs

If you want to produce your own chicks but have neither a cockerel to produce fertile eggs nor a broody to hatch them out, you will need a supply of fertile eggs from an outside source, and an incubator.

Some older models of incubator work on the principle of an oil lamp heating a water tank to provide the right heat for hatching. Most modern types, however, are heated by an electric element controlled by a thermostatic switch. They are all supplied with instructions which, if followed closely, will result in success. The best incubator in the world is only as good as the eggs inside, and the operator.

The correct temperature during incubation is vital and you

will have to turn the eggs at least three times a day by hand, a process which would normally be done by the sitting hen, to prevent the chick embryo sticking to the inside of the shell. Some models of incubator have automatic turning devices but they generally cost more. The size of incubator depends on how many eggs you plan to hatch. Some have a capacity of twenty-five hen eggs (half that if you want to hatch goose eggs) and others can hold up to two hundred eggs.

Incubators can sometimes be bought second-hand, or you might be able to borrow one, but a new one will give years of good service and will, in all probability, prove a worthwhile investment.

Acquiring fertile eggs might be a problem but by now you may have made contact with other poultry-keepers who should be able to suggest a source. Roadside produce stalls sometimes have fertile eggs for sale, so do vets in some rural areas. Check the small advertisements in the local paper, too.

The choice of eggs is important. Use good size, clean eggs from hens rather than pullets. They should be about $2\frac{1}{2}$ oz and not more than a week old after which hatchability tends to decline rapidly. The fresher the egg the better. Avoid using very large eggs. It hatching your own eggs you may be very proud that your hens are laying super-size eggs but they could be double-yolkers and unlikely to hatch anyway. Avoid misshapen or cracked eggs, even a hairline crack can allow infection to enter, and do not wash the eggs before putting them in the incubator. Cleanliness is a decided virtue in most aspects of poultry keeping but not when it comes to setting hatching eggs. Washing destroys the mucin on the shell and this could allow germs to enter the shell through minute pores. Instead gently brush off any dirt. If the eggs have to be stored before setting keep them broad end up in fibre egg trays at a temperature of between 50° and 55°F/10° and 13°C, turning them twice a day. A tray of water nearby will help to prevent the eggs dehydrating.

Before placing them in the incubator mark an X on one side only which will help when it comes to turning and mark the date that they are due to hatch. The incubation period for a hen egg is twenty-one days, although not all the chicks will hatch at once.

Do not overload the incubator with too many eggs, and make sure that the water tray which will be at the bottom beneath the

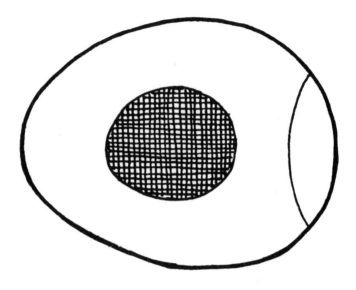

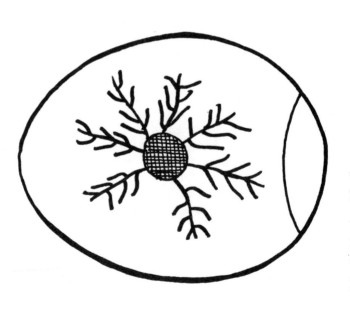

Infertile (clear) and fertile eggs

egg tray is topped up to ensure adequate moisture. Some models have a sponge layer instead which needs to be kept damp. For hens' eggs humidity needs to be around 60 per cent, and this can be measured with a hygrometer. Moisture prevents excessive drying out of the natural moisture in the egg but if the incubator is being operated in a damp room, like a cellar, then extra moisture may not be needed. Ensure that the incubator is firm and level and in a room of between 65° and 70°F/18° and 21°C which is free of draughts and violent changes in temperature which might be caused by sunlight, central heating or an open fire. Follow the manufacturer's instructions carefully on the correct hatching temperature which will be measured by a thermometer inside the apparatus.

Testing for Fertility

After seven or eight days in the incubator test the eggs for fertility by shining a light through them, a process which is known as 'candling' because originally the eggs were tested using candlelight. Proprietary gadgets are available to do this but you can make your own by screwing a bulb holder onto a square piece of wood and placing an inverted tin, with a hole about $1\frac{1}{4}$ inch in diameter cut out of the top, over the holder. The egg for testing is then placed over the hole, the bulb (60 watt) is switched on and any other light in the room turned off. The eggs will have to be taken from the incubator one by one to do this, so work fairly quickly to avoid chilling the other eggs.

Infertile eggs will show up as perfectly clear; an egg that appears thick and cloudy is one in which the embryo has started to incubate but has died; fertile eggs contain small spidery veins radiating from a dark red centre. Candling also shows up the air sac at the broad end of the egg which provides oxygen for the developing chick before hatching.

Eggs that are clear or cloudy should be removed and replaced with fresh eggs. The clear eggs can be hard boiled and fed back to the hens or any chicks from an earlier hatch although some people eat them themselves.

Hatching

Most incubators have a plastic see-through panel on the top so that you can see what, if anything, is happening inside. For most of the time this will be precisely nothing. Cease turning the eggs on the nineteenth day and at this stage, by holding the eggs to your ear, you should be able to hear the chicks 'pipping' the shell ready for hatching. 'Pipping' is the name given to the chicks' repeated tapping of the shell, and the chicks will continue to do this until a perforation line has been made around the shell.

On the twentieth day chips should be appearing on the shell, so make sure the eggs are turned chipped side up. The chick will continue chipping right round the perforation until it can force the two halves of the shell apart. This is the time when young children, and possibly their parents as well, will be reluctant to leave the incubator, but make sure that in the excitement of watching the painstaking progress of the new arrivals the incubator is not knocked. Any vibration can damage unhatched chicks.

All being well, by the twenty-first day the chicks should be out and at first they will present a fairly pathetic picture. They will be weak, wet and exhausted and totally unlike the fluffy, busy little things the beginner might have imagined. But leave them alone for twenty-four hours, giving them time to dry off, and they will look completely different. They can then be lifted gently out of the incubator and transferred to the brooder which should have been warmed up beforehand. Eggs still in the incubator and not pipping by the twenty-second day should be discarded. The golden rule about hatching eggs in an incubator is to leave well alone; do not interfere with a chick that is hatching because you may injure it.

Success rates will vary: twenty-five fertile eggs may not result in twenty-five chicks. Fatalities can be caused by a number of factors, of which incorrect temperature and moisture levels are high on the list, but hen eggs are much easier to hatch than the eggs of waterfowl.

Chicks can also be born deformed and blind and are best killed as soon as possible after hatching. One way of doing this is to break the chick's neck by pressing it firmly against a sharp-edged piece of wood like a door frame. Some people tap them on the head. Either way you may find the business of killing a newly-hatched chick distressing, but there is no point in rearing birds with deformities. If you can't face the prospect of doing it yourself then call in a fellow poultry-keeper to do the job for you. Thankfully nature has a way of taking over, and deformed chicks often die during hatching. Beware of power cuts when incubating eggs. A sudden plunge in temperature will chill the eggs in an electric incubator – which may be one factor in favour of incubators running on paraffin.

Keep a sleeping bag or a pile of blankets handy to throw over the incubator during a power cut. This will retain some of the heat but remember to take any covering off again when power is restored and the incubator starts warming up again otherwise it may catch fire and that could mean more to worry about than a few roasted chicks.

Fostering With a Broody Hen

Instead of transferring the day-old chicks to an artificial brooder you could try placing them under a broody hen who has previously been housed in a coop with a run attached.

Pullets are unreliable as broodies. The best broody is a hen that is two years old or over. Generally the pure breeds and cross breeds from them make the most suitable broodies. The 'heavy' breeds like the Rhode Island and the Light Sussex are more likely to go broody than the 'light' breeds. The broody should sit on dummy eggs – known as china eggs or pot eggs – for a week to ensure her broodiness and make sure that the coop where she will rear her foster chicks is separated from non-broody hens, because they may disturb the chicks and the broody.

Introducing the chicks is best done after dark. Put one of the chicks under the broody and wait for her reaction. What you are asking the broody to do is to accept something that she knows she has not hatched herself, and not all broodies are ready to accept half-truths. She may accept the chick after a minute or two – in fact she probably will; but there is a chance that she will literally kick it out with her feet in which case you will have to revert to some sort of artificial brooder.

Assuming that she accepts the chick happily, let her have the rest one by one. They will quickly disappear beneath the broody's fluffed out feathers and she will probably cluck her satisfaction at having a ready-made family. One of the larger breeds like the Rhode Island or the Light Sussex (or a cross of the two) will happily foster a dozen chicks.

Feed the chicks with chopped up hard boiled egg, breadcrumbs or proprietary chick-crumbs. This is best carried out in the coop where the hen will quickly teach the chicks how to peck. Again, tapping the food tray might help. Later the chicks can be allowed out into the adjoining wire run to forage for scattered chick crumbs and greenstuff. Water is essential.

Some poultrymen restrict the broody to the coop with bars, allowing only the chicks access to the run. But it seems unkind – and unnecessary – to deny the broody the freedom to walk around with her foster chicks. The worst she can do is to scratch up the grass but, if the coop and run are moved regularly, the problem of an unsightly lawn is minimized. The coop should be situated so that it is protected from high winds and affords adequate shelter. It should also be secure at night from attacks by rats, cats, stoats, polecats and anything else that might take a fancy to young chicks.

Do not forget the needs of the broody hen during the initial rearing. She needs feeding too, so give her some mixed corn or layer's pellets – preferably in a trough where the chicks cannot get at it. If the hen and her chicks are to go free-range and there are no other older hens around, then let them out after three or four weeks, and they will return to the coop each night. If there are other older hens this will have to be postponed for a few more weeks – even if it means creating a larger temporary pen. The chicks may be attacked and generally harrassed by the older birds, and the poor old broody will be working overtime trying to protect her charges. The other problem is that the chicks may pick up disease from ground used by other stock.

When the chicks are about six or seven weeks old the foster mother can then be taken out and returned to the laying flock and brought back into lay again. She may have already started laying again anyway. The maternal instinct will have worn off by this time and the separation will be no hardship either to the foster mother or the chicks.

Hatching With a Broody
If you have a hen that has gone broody, preferably around March or April so that the new pullets will be coming into lay during the autumn, then let her hatch out a clutch of eggs and

save yourself the trouble, work and expense of an incubator.

Again, make sure that she really is broody by trying her on a few dummy eggs. The same advice on the choice of eggs applies as before — well-shaped, good size, no cracks. If the eggs are dirty, gently brush off the worst of the dirt but do not wash them.

The broody hen has got to sit on the eggs for three weeks, so make the nest as comfortable as possible and in a quiet, semi-dark spot well away from possible disturbance from other hens, cats, dogs and inquisitive children. Make the nest in a box about eighteen inches deep. Place a turf 3-4 in thick, grass side down, on the bottom of the box. Make a saucer-shaped shallow depression in the soil and line the nest with good quality hay or straw which is mould-free. The soil, which will be slightly damp, will provide humidity during the incubation period.

Place the broody gently on the eggs at night. Do not give her too many because she may not be able to cover them all in comfort. If your broody is one of the 'heavy' breeds then let her sit on a dozen eggs. During the sitting the hen will rotate the eggs under her and, if there are too many, some on the outside of the circle may get chilled.

Opinions vary as to the management of a sitting hen. Some say make sure that she is off the nest for ten minutes each day to feed, exercise and attend to the calls of nature. For the first few days until she gets the hang of it this will mean lifting her off the nest and putting her back on. The other theory is to leave her alone with an adequate supply of food and water (both of which will need regular changing) within reach and letting her get on with it. You can also give her a supply of grit and fresh greens and a dust bath too.

In my experience the less disturbance the better; too much may cause her to leave the eggs. In a free-range flock of hens running with a cockerel, chances are a hen will go broody and hatch out a clutch of eggs and the first you will know about it is when she returns with a bright new fluffy family at foot. No incubator, no brooder, no candling. When all is said and done hens know quite a bit about hatching. The broody hen probably will not leave the nest for more than five or ten minutes at a time but in fact the eggs will not come to any harm if she remains off for twice as long. Although she may have a supply of food nearby she will drastically reduce her intake and lose a lot of condition in the process. But the nest-box slim-in reduces her own body-weight and the risk of her crushing either the eggs or the newly-hatched chicks.

During the third week of incubation the eggs can be splashed with warm water once a day while the broody is off the nest to raise the humidity, but when hatching is due after twenty-one days, leave the broody well alone. It takes up to ten hours for a chick to hatch from the moment the first chip in the shell appears. Not all the chicks will hatch at the same time, and after the first has hatched the hen will remain sitting on the others. If you can do so easily without getting pecked (sitting hens can become very protective) remove the empty shells, after the first few chicks are out, to prevent possible injury. The hatching rate may be only 70 to 80 per cent and, when all the eggs that are going to hatch have done so, leave the chicks alone with the broody for a few hours giving them time to dry off and then transfer them all to a previously prepared coop and run.

Breaking a Hen of Broodiness

If a hen has gone broody and you do not want her to sit on eggs she can be 'broken' of broodiness by being put in a coop by herself but within sight of other hens. After a few days she will decide for herself that scratching outside with the rest is far better than being cooped-up playing at make-believe-mother and will demonstrate her anxiety by trying to get out through the bars of the run. Take her out and put her back with the other hens.

Sex Linkage

One of the problems about hatching eggs with a broody or an incubator is that there are no guarantees about the sex of the chicks, and you may end up with two pullets and ten cockerels. That is no problem if you wish to rear cockerels in a separate pen for the table, and have the time and the space to do it, but it could be a problem if both are limited.

Reducing uncertainty completely is one of the advantages of buying in chicks which are 'sex linked', a method of cross-breeding which enables the sex of chicks to be determined at one day old. In sex linking the colour of the offspring and the sex are linked in certain crosses. The sex is determined by the female through the dominant characteristics on her sex chromosome, which means that a brown cockerel (say a Rhode Island Red) crossed with a white hen (a light Sussex for example) can produce white cockerels and brown pullets.

Sex-linkage saves commercial breeders the expense of rearing unwanted cockerels. Sometimes you may see adverts for chicks 'as hatched' in which the sex is not guaranteed and it is a question of pot-luck, but chicks bought this way are generally cheaper.

Whatever way you choose to obtain replacement pullets they will need to be kept separate from older birds during rearing, and problems may occur if the two flocks are merged into one after the pullets have started to lay. Separation of pullets from second year birds is important because if kept as one flock the pullets may get pushed to the back of the queue at feeding time while the older, but less productive, birds overeat. The pullets may also be attacked by the older birds and may not lay well as a result.

Is It Worth Keeping a Cockerel?

If you have only a few hens in a back garden the answer is a definite 'no'. Keeping a cockerel does not lead to any increase in egg production, and introducing a cockerel to birds that have neither seen nor heard one in their life before can only disturb them, and may put them off lay.

Cockerels like to indulge their natural inclinations – often preferring the afternoons to mornings – but in a confined space this may lead to nothing more than continual rape. Feeding costs must also be considered, although a gentleman cockerel will let his wives have first go at the feeding troughs, and make do with any leftovers. And, not everyone likes being woken at dawn, or even earlier, by a cockerel. There is a theory that putting a cockerel in a low roofed building – or on a high perch immediately below the roof – stops the 'cock-a-doodle-do' because he has not got the space to stretch his neck and point his beak upwards, both of which are pre-requisites to the sound-making, but I cannot vouch for the effectiveness of this noise-control measure. My own thinking is that if you want a cockerel you should be prepared to put up with whatever noise he wants to make — although as an alarm clock he may be totally unreliable.

The only real benefit from keeping a cockerel is a supply of fertile eggs for hatching. Any cockerel of ten months or older will do the job, but make sure that he is not closely related to the hens because inbreeding may result in chick deformities.

You may be able to pick up a cockerel from a market, but for a top quality gentleman go to a breeder. Make sure the cockerel has been vaccinated against Fowl Pest and do not put him in with too many hens otherwise the poor chap will get run down and a large proportion of infertile eggs will result. Neither should the cockerel be put in with pullets if you want good hatching eggs. The chances of a good percentage of fertile eggs increases the longer the cockerel is with the hens, but leave it for about a month before taking any eggs for hatching.

Fertility begins to decline in a cockerel after five or six years but by then, if he has done his job well, he will have given rise to dozens of good quality chicks, many of which will be dead long before his own time is up. It is a tough world.

7

KILLING FOR THE TABLE

This is the bit which puts a lot of people off, and if you really cannot stomach the thought of killing a hen or cockerel that you may have reared from one day old (or even seen hatch out) then get an experienced poultry-keeper to do the job for you. There is no shame in being 'chicken', and it is far better to get someone who knows what he is doing rather than making a mess of the job yourself.

Decision time for the hens comes after two laying seasons (or after one season if you are going to be ruthlessly efficient about what should be a simple and pleasurable hobby) when the number of eggs will start to decline, although they will be larger. If you want to keep them longer, then go ahead. I know farmers who have kept hens pottering around the place until they have simply pegged out through old age.

After two laying seasons a hen is not a very saleable item alive. It is worth more to you as meat which may seem an unkind way of repaying a hen for all her hard work and months of valuable service, but that is a fact of life. Hens or cockerels can be fattened for the table on a proprietary food called broiler finisher. If the hens have been free-range, confine them to a run or they will run off the extra weight gained. Give them mixed corn too, as much as they will clear up in ten minutes, and any spare milk you have to make the flesh white and more succulent.

Some poultry-keepers confine the doomed birds to a semi-dark house during fattening, which is supposed to make them convert food into meat more efficiently, but if that strikes you as being too much like factory farming then don't do it. In any case do not feed the birds for the last twelve hours. This is not an economy measure but rather ensures that the last meal has passed through the body before killing. If you have reared a separate pen of cockerels these will be ready for killing at about five or six months, possibly earlier. A cockerel of ten-months old is about the maximum if you want to roast it. Commercially some cockerels are caponized, which means they have a hormone pellet inserted under the skin of the neck. This causes the testes to shrink in size and activity, the bird puts on weight quicker and the flesh is more tender. It also stops confined males from fighting each other, an exercise which uses up energy which should be going into the production of meat instead.

Killing is best done by dislocating the bird's head from the neck, so snapping the spinal cord. This is what you do: firmly grasp the bird's legs and wing tips in the left hand and put the first two fingers of the right hand behind the head. Holding the bird downwards across the right knee exert pressure with the right hand until you feel the spinal cord snap and the head loosen. It requires a jerk and a twist at the same time. It is easier said than done, and if you can get someone with experience to show you how to do it for the first few times, so much the better. As in all things, practice makes perfect.

Once the spinal cord has been broken the bird feels no pain but keep a tight hold because it may flap its wings violently for a few minutes. The bird is by now quite dead, and the flapping and twisting is caused by nerves. There is another way of killing which is achieved by holding the neck of the bird on a block of wood and chopping off the head with a very sharp axe in one fell swoop like a guillotine. I know a country vicar who regularly does it this way but it is messy, bloody and carries the inbuilt danger of slicing your hand off. Dislocation is much safer. Commercial producers stun the birds first with an electric 'wand' before dislocation.

Plucking
The bird should be plucked immediately while it is still warm when the feathers come out easier. Sit on a low chair or stool, hold the legs and wings with the head dangling down away from you and start plucking the back feathers using the thumb and first finger. The idea is to pluck quickly without pulling too many feathers at one go. Pulling too many at once might tear

the skin which does not look very nice if you are selling oven-ready birds. When the back is finished turn the bird over and pluck the breast (some people start on the breast first) and then the neck, legs and finally the tail feathers. Hang the bird overnight in a place free from flies to allow the blood to drain into the neck.

Drawing

Next day prepare the bird for the oven or freezer: place the plucked bird on its back on a work surface and take hold of the skin of the throat. With a sharp knife cut the skin all around the neck just below the head. Pull the skin away from the neck as far as you can and ease away the windpipe, which is transparent and quite firm, from the neck.

Hold the windpipe low down and pull it out of the chest until it breaks. Ease away the soft food pipe from the neck following its course with your finger into the chest and, gradually easing the stomach out, cut the pipe leading from the stomach as far down as possible. Then pull the head off and discard this along with the two pipes and the stomach. Cut the neck off as close to the shoulders as you can and retain for giblets. Fold the flap of skin neatly over the neck hole and down the bird's back folding the wings back onto themselves to hold the flap in place.

Then turn to the legs. Cut through the skin around the hocks. Bend the joint backwards until it snaps and, still holding the foot, pull out the ligaments throwing them and the feet away. The ligaments may be very hard to pull out, and if this is too difficult then cut them out as neatly as you can. Bend the legs up by the side of the bird and with a sharp knife pierce the skin in the centre just below the rib cage and above the vent.

Gradually work the skin away from the guts with your fingers and cut the skin around the vent being careful not to cut the guts. Insert your hand into this hole and gradually ease the innards away from the carcass and remove them completely. You can then see the lungs lying high up on the ribs. Remove these by sliding your finger under them and throw them away. The heart, gizzard and liver can be kept along with the neck for giblets. The gizzard must be cleaned first by cutting half way through it with a knife, pulling out the yellow bag of grit and discarding it.

Wipe the inside of the bird clean with a damp cloth and singe the carcass to remove fluff and hairs. This can be done with a burning piece of paper or by holding the carcass over a lighted gas jet.

8

STORAGE AND SALE OF EGGS

At certain times of year, especially during the spring and summer, you may have more eggs than the family requires. The surplus can either be stored for use in low-production periods later, or sold. Although eggs are best used fresh they can be preserved for months and yet still retain much of their goodness. Eggs for storage should be as fresh as possible – it does eggs no good at all to be allowed to remain uncollected in dirty nest boxes. To test eggs for freshness put them in a bowl of water – fresh eggs sink, bad ones float. Whole eggs will keep for two to three weeks in a cool, dry larder and for up to four weeks in a fridge at 40°F/4°C. Shelled, beaten up and put in plastic bags in the freezer (three or four eggs to each bag) they will keep for about sixteen months and, once thawed, the mixture can be used for making omelettes, cakes and for other cookery. Eggs cannot be stored in the freezer still in their shells because they would burst on freezing. If preserved in the freezer they should be thawed out completely before being used and this will take about nine hours if they are removed from the freezer to the fridge, and four hours at room temperature. After thawing they should be used as soon as possible.

Whole yolks last for a day in a larder, four to five days in a fridge (in water) and two months in a freezer (with salt or sugar added). White keep for one week in the fridge and six months in the freezer. Hard-boiled eggs keep for four to five days in a fridge and indefinitely in a freezer.

The freezer revolution has made food preservation a simple process but, even without a freezer, surplus eggs can still be preserved by sealing the pores in the egg shell so that air and harmful bacteria are excluded. Eggs to be preserved like this should be free of any cracks and clean, but not washed, because this would remove the protective coating on the shell.

One way of sealing the shell is to coat it with water-glass – a solution of sodium silicate powder and water which is obtainable at some chemists. Dilute the solution as directed and pour it over the eggs packed in layers in an enamel or galvanized bucket with their small ends pointing downwards. Make sure the eggs are well covered. Put a lid on the bucket and keep it in a cool room. More eggs can be added as long as the solution is kept topped up. Eggs will keep in water-glass for up to six months but, when removed for use, will need washing to remove the sticky white film caused by the solution. They can then be used in the same way as fresh eggs except for boiling because storage in the solution tends to soften the shells.

Instead of water-glass, limewater can be used made up from two parts slaked lime and one part salt to sixteen parts water, although the eggs will not keep as long. Another way to preserve eggs is to rub the shells all over with melted dripping or lard to seal the pores. The eggs are then stored pointed ends down in egg boxes or in a tin without a lid, and will keep for up to nine months.

Clean, new-laid eggs can be coated with a solution of gum arabic made from equal parts of gum and water. The top half of the egg should be painted first and left to dry before doing the bottom half. Eggs painted with two coats of gum arabic have kept satisfactorily for six months.

Salt is one of the cheapest ways of preserving eggs. Use normal cooking salt, dry it in the oven first and then cool it. Stack the eggs in layers in a container (wooden barrels have been much used for this) putting an inch of salt between each layer. Preservation time is about six months.

Pickling is another way of preserving. Boil the eggs for ten minutes and put them in cold water. Remove the shells and put the eggs in jars of spiced vinegar. The jars should have tight fitting lids. Eggs pickled in this way are often sold in pubs.

Even egg shells have their uses, apart from baking and crushing them up for your hens. Egg shells can help remove discolouration from glass water bottles and decanters by being crushed up and shaken in the bottle in warm, soapy water. A mixture of finely crushed shells and ordinary salt is useful in getting rid of stains on enamelware. Winemakers, also, sometimes use finely-ground shells for clearing cloudy wine.

Grading Eggs

There was a time when eggs were sold in the U.K. as large (approx $2\frac{1}{4}$ oz) standard (2 oz) or medium ($1\frac{3}{4}$ oz) but that has since changed with our entering the Common Market. Eggs are now sold in seven E.E.C. sizes.

These are:

> Size 1 : Eggs weighing 70g ($2\frac{1}{2}$ oz) and over
> Size 2: Eggs weighing 65-70g ($2\frac{1}{4}$-$2\frac{1}{2}$ oz)
> Size 3: Eggs weighing 60-65g (2-$2\frac{1}{4}$ oz)
> Size 4: Eggs weighing 55-60g ($1\frac{7}{8}$-2 oz)
> Size 5: Eggs weighing 50-55g ($1\frac{3}{4}$-$1\frac{7}{8}$ oz)
> Size 6: Eggs weighing 45-50g ($1\frac{1}{2}$-$1\frac{3}{4}$ oz)
> Size 7: Eggs weighing under 45g ($1\frac{1}{2}$ oz)

Producers can be prosecuted if the eggs being sold are incorrectly labelled, but the domestic poultryman selling his surplus eggs door-to-door, at the farm gate, or on a market stall is exempt from these weight provisions. Grade your surplus eggs as you like – from little to big to super-big. The sale price depends on you, but remember that eggs from free-range hens generally carry a premium over all other eggs. As a price guide check what the local health food shop is charging for its non-battery eggs. Make sure that any eggs you offer for sale are as fresh as possible, so mark each egg with the date it was laid and store them on fibre trays which hold thirty eggs.

Try to ensure, also, that your eggs for sale are top quality. Commercially there are three classifications of egg quality:

A: fresh eggs, naturally clean, shell intact, internally perfect. The air sac must not exceed 6mm.

B: downgraded for reasons such as staleness, internal meat or blood spots or because the eggs have been preserved in some way. The air sac must not exceed 9mm.

C: These eggs cannot be sold to the public.

Try to make your own eggs for sale 'A' class too – free of hairline cracks in the shell and blood spots inside caused by a slight rupture of blood vessels as the egg is being formed in the oviduct. There is nothing harmful about either blood or meat spots, they just do not look very pleasant when the egg is freshly cracked.

To check for quality candle the eggs with the candling device mentioned earlier, or shine a torch through the egg in a dark room.

Incorrect storing of surplus eggs for sale might result in an old egg being included in a batch of allegedly 'new laid' and that could mean the loss of both your customers and your reputation.

Keeping Accounts

Keeping detailed records of your poultry enterprise is not essential, and accountancy may not be your strong point anyway. I once had a farmer friend who kept hens for twenty years without having a clue what his eggs were costing. He fed them bread discarded by a local cafe and the cheapest wheat he could get and my guess is that it would have been far cheaper for him to have bought his eggs at the local shop.

It is useful to know how your hens and your pocket are faring financially, and this does not mean drawing up a huge and complicated set of accounts. Concentrate on operating costs first – the initial cost of the birds, the feed bill for twenty months and any extras like the cost of winter lighting to maintain production in winter. Lighting will probably have to be estimated. A 60 watt bulb uses about one unit in seventeen hours, so the cost of that will be minimal.

The returns side of the ledger will include the number of eggs laid in a year, the income from the sale of surplus eggs and, if any, the value of home-produced meat. If all has gone well your eggs should be costing less than those from the supermarket. It is difficult to say precisely how much less, for that will depend on a number of factors: the quality of the stock, feeding, the level of your own management and so on.

It will also depend to what degree you can cut feeding costs for the hens by providing food from the garden, and whether you have access to a supply of cheap bread – like my farmer friend. The poultryman in a rural area may also be able to explore other cost-cutting avenues denied to his suburban counterpart. Some large-scale farmers, for example, buy wheat in 10-ton lots for on-the-farm mixing for livestock. They get their wheat cheaper because they buy in bulk. Obtaining wheat from a friendly farmer may certainly be cheaper than buying it yourself at the local agricultural merchants. So stay on good terms with farmers in the vicinity. Even buying one ton of wheat or mixed corn direct from the merchants yourself will be cheaper than buying in separate 55 lb sacks from the same place – provided of course you have the storage space.

But if you cannot cut the cost of bought-in food, then pay the bill and keep smiling: your eggs should still be cheaper than at the shop and they will certainly be fresher. The temptation for the newcomer to poultry-keeping is to start working out costs when the young pullets have been laying for only a few weeks, but this gives a totally false picture with the eggs costing a few pence each and this situation unfortunately will not last.

When the colder weather comes the birds will lay less and, worse still, some of the stock may be lost through ill-health or the attacks of predators. To get a true picture of the economics of poultry-keeping wait for a full laying season before doing any sums. If you are keeping the birds for two laying seasons and then despatching them to the freezer and buying in point-of-lay replacements the accountancy will be fairly simple. But if you rear your own then other costs will have to go into the equation such as the cost of buying day-old chicks or, if hatching eggs, the running costs of the incubator, the heat used in rearing, and feeding costs.

The capital costs in setting up the unit – hen house, wire runs, feeders and drinkers – will largely depend on how much do-it-yourself was involved. But these costs can largely be ignored because if and when the time comes that you want to cease poultry-keeping then the equipment can be sold for not much less than the original cost.

If you want to complete the costs and returns exercise you could always set the capital costs against a theoretical income by comparing the costs of your own eggs with shop prices over a period of say three or four years.

It is difficult to cost out all aspects of poultry keeping, anyway. How do you cost out in monetary terms the benefit of poultry manure on your garden or even, come to that, resting your head on a feather pillow at night? And such thoughts bring us on to muck and feathers. Hens not only provide eggs, they also produce a first rate organic fertilizer for the vegetable garden. The average hen produces about one hundredweight of droppings a year which is slightly more than the weight of food consumed in the same period. This manure is richer in nitrogen, phosphate and potash than farmyard manure.

The poultryman keeping hens either free-range or in movable units is at an advantage because poultry manure is at its best as a fertilizer when the droppings fall directly onto the land. Losses of nitrogen to the atmosphere are minimized and if the runs are moved frequently this distributes the manure over a wide area and so improves poor grassland with no work and at a very low cost. The domestic poultryman is unlikely to have any poor grassland requiring this tonic treatment, but even he can put the manure to very good use. Chicken manure can be stored under cover to prevent rain washing out valuable nitrogen for spreading on the garden in the spring or for adding to the compost heap where it helps to rot down vegetable waste and so improves the fertilizing value of the compost. Old hen-house litter like chopped straw, peat moss, wood shavings, can also be added to the compost although manures containing large amounts of litter are less beneficial to the soil.

Poultry manure can be forked into the vegetable garden during the spring at about 4 oz to the square yard but it should not be mixed with lime or basic slag (a waste product from steelworks used by farmers as a low-cost fertilizer) because this leads to a loss of valuable nitrogen.

Chicken feathers will also help to rot down compost or they can be used for stuffing pillows after first being dried in a slow oven.

There are other aspects of poultry keeping which also defy the costing out exercise. How do you cost out your own time and the enjoyment in feeding and collecting eggs and generally caring for the stock? And if these things are not enjoyable, if they have become a daily and weekly drudge, then it is time to stop. And that is roughly where we came in. Keep poultry because you want to. If the idea of a freshly laid egg still warm from the nest makes your pulse quicken, then get cracking.

9

DUCKS

Ducks are healthy, hardy creatures and full of character – much more so than chickens. They are also independent, comical, entertaining and a joy to keep. The champion egg laying breeds, the well-known Khaki Campbell and the less well known Welsh Harlequin, average 300 eggs a year, which is more than a hen can manage on average, and the eggs are heavier with more protein and less water.

Drakes can also be fattened for the table quicker than cocks with one of the main meat breeds, the Aylesbury, able to reach 6 lb liveweight in under eight weeks. The housing needs of both layers and table birds are simple, and cooked potatoes and greenfood can make up a large proportion of the diet.

So, why don't more people keep ducks? The answer lies in the size of the average back garden. Even half a dozen ducks need a grazing area of about 50 ft x 50 ft and that is usually beyond the capabilities of the suburban garden. Ducks can be confined to a smaller area but they do not thrive as well, quite apart from the fact that it is unkind to imprison ducks, or any other domestic creature for that matter, in an area that is too small.

As a general rule, each duck needs 10 sq ft of run space and, as with hens, having two runs is better than one because this is more beneficial to the ducks and to the ground being grazed.

Duck eggs have never been as popular as hen eggs, partly because of the lingering suspicion that duck eggs can harbour poisons. It is certainly true that duck eggs are more prone to picking up disease organisms because of the relatively large pores in the shell. But if the eggs are being laid in clean nests and are collected regularly this reduces the disease risk to practically nil, as with hen eggs. Duck eggs, however, do not keep as well as hen eggs, again because of their more porous shells, and are best used within seven to ten days after being stored at about 50°F/10°C. The taste of duck eggs is stronger than hen eggs, but many people prefer them.

Because of the space problem ducks are not really recommended for suburban back gardens, but if the garden is large enough or if you live on a smallholding with a field or two, then the keeping of ducks will bring a great deal of pleasure with some profit thrown in. There are exceptions to every rule but generally ducks, well-housed and adequately fed, will wander around at peace with the world giving the odd quack. Geese, who have a totally unjustified reputation for viciousness, can be used as watchdogs but ducks never!

Ducks enjoy swimming and washing, and while a pond is not vital they do need a receptacle deep enough to allow them to cover their heads completely. Nose and eye troubles may occur if they cannot do this. However, if you intend breeding with ducks, swimming water is desirable to ensure successful mating, especially with the heavier breeds because the added buoyancy of the water helps the drake to mount the duck.

Ducks are long-lived creatures – up to ten years in some cases, although the average is four or five – but as with hens there comes a time when it is no longer profitable to keep them. Egg production drops by about 25 per cent in the second year's lay, with a similar drop the following year, but it does pay to keep ducks for one laying season longer than hens despite the fact that they eat more food.

Check any local regulations before you start and if there are neighbours around think of them too. If not kept properly duck housing can smell, as can dirty ducks.

Housing Ducks

Duck housing can be either bought or made, or a disused building can be adapted. Nothing elaborate is needed but the more space the better. Do not confine them to a leaking packing case. Housing can be very simple but it also needs to be draught-proof, well-ventilated and proof against vermin. Each duck needs a minimum floor space of 3 sq ft, but ducks do not perch at night so the house need not be very tall – say 4 ft at the front sloping to 3 ft at the back. The slope will shed rainwater, and if

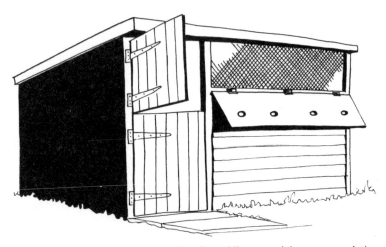

Example of an 8' x 6' house capable of providing overnight accommodation for ten ducks or six geese

this is run off in guttering to a water butt it can be used in the garden later. It is good practice to have a decent overhang all round the shed roof of three or four inches because this helps to throw water away from the house and so keep it dry along with the area of run nearest to it.

Regular jobs like egg collection are made much easier if the top of the house is either hinged or can be lifted off completely. There is no point in having a house that you have got to crawl inside to retrieve the eggs. Not only will this be a dirty and difficult duty, it may also upset the ducks in any nearby run and ducks dislike excitement even more than hens.

Having a hinged or lift-off top also helps to air the house in fine weather, drying out any damp litter. Ducks loathe damp and will soon indicate if their housing is unattractive by refusing to go in at night. Like geese they are prone to rheumatism. The floor of the house can be of slatted timber, concrete or half-inch galvanized wire on a stout timber frame so that the wire is a few inches off the ground. Solid wooden floors have the disadvantage of being permanently wet and earth floors are not advisable because rats, one of the main enemies of both ducklings and ducks, can quickly tunnel up into the house. Rats can also be a problem with slatted or wire floors.

Possible solutions are to raise the house a few inches off the ground on legs with metal 'rat baffles' on each leg or to bury sheets of corrugated iron around the house at a depth of two or three feet. Either of these methods should be successful – but rats are pretty determined creatures especially when they know that there are ducks (or hens) around. Concrete is the real answer to foil rats, although a concrete floor needs a greater depth of litter.

The doorway of the duckhouse is much more important than on a hen house. Compared with ducks, hens are orderly creatures and will hop out one-by-one when unlocked each day, but ducks have far less patience and will try to jam up the doorway in the rush to get out. If you intend keeping half a dozen ducks then make the doorway 2 ft wide to enable two ducks to get out at the same time. If the house is raised off the ground the ducks will need a ramp to get out otherwise they may jump out and even a drop of a few inches can lead to injured legs and possible lameness. Put wooden ribs horizontally across the ramp to stop clumsy ducks falling off.

Dry bedding for ducks is essential and floor litter can be peat, sawdust or well-chopped straw. Peat is the most expensive but will benefit the garden most when the time comes to renew the litter. Like chicken manure a mixture of duck droppings and soiled litter makes a useful fertilizer in the vegetable patch, but keep it for a few months first letting it weather on the compost or dung heap before use. Duck manure is too strong for raw application.

If the bedding becomes smelly or damp then renew it. There are different ideas as to the best method of littering a duck house. One is that any damp litter can be topped up with fresh, dry material making a deep-litter requiring removal once every six months by which time it may be twelve inches thick and compressed hard by the pressure of the ducks' feet. The other idea is to clean out the litter religiously every week, thoroughly cleaning the house at the same time.

It is up to you which method you adopt but make sure the litter stays as dry as possible, and clean, to prevent eggs becoming soiled through lying on a dirty floor. If the deep-litter system is to be used then a board will be needed at the bottom of the ducks' doorway to stop the litter spilling out into the run. Windows are not required in a small duck house but wire grilles should be built in to provide sufficient ventilation. Duck housing must not be stuffy.

If adapting an existing building which has windows, then block some of them off with hardboard panels or sacking. Too much light in the house can cause the inmates to panic and that could lead to an outburst of early morning quacking which may not make you too popular with any close neighbours.

Intricate nest boxes are not required either. Ducks will lay their eggs happily on the floor of the house among the litter, but it is better to make a small area of straw at one end of the house, keeping the straw in place with a line of housebricks or a piece of heavy timber. This nesting straw can then be replaced without renewing the rest of the litter.

Siting the duck house is as important as it is with a hen house, and the best position is on a slight, well-drained slope to keep the house and adjoining runs as dry as possible. Face the house south or south-east so that it gets all the sun possible – sunlight helps to dry any moisture taken into the house by the ducks. Ventilation grilles and the door should face away from prevailing winds.

The Duck Run

If you have a smallholding then a duck run will probably not be necessary. Let the ducks free-range and they will forage for a lot of their own food. Ducks are in fact more efficient at foraging than hens, and less destructive, but you had better still keep them out of the vegetable garden. If they are to be kept in a large garden then some form of penning is obviously necessary.

Ducks do very well on land that would be too wet for most other stock, but they will still turn a small run into a quagmire if restricted to it all the time. One alternative is to have one grassed run and another smaller concreted area for use in very wet weather. To confine the ducks to a pen it will be necessary to clip their wings, although this does not apply to all breeds – the Aylesbury, for example, is too heavy for flight.

Get someone to show you how to clip the wings. It is best done during the first ten days of life by cutting the last quarter inch off one wing with a sharp knife. In older stock the top $2\frac{1}{2}$ in of the flight feathers of one wing can be removed with very sharp scissors. Both operations are harmless and painless but they do require skill, so get someone who knows how to do it, rather than make a mess of the job yourself, possibly causing discomfort to the ducks. Clipping is done on one wing only because the idea is to throw the bird off her natural flight balance. Clipping both wings would tend to defeat the object.

The netting for any run needs to be 3 ft high and of small mesh, not large enough for a duck to get its head through or it may be decapitated by a fox.

During day-time ducks need some shade from hot sun, so incorporate small trees or bushes in the run. If this is not possible try to arrange shade from a fence or wall when siting the run, or even use a few sheets of corrugated iron. The house itself will cast some shadow, of course, and making this part of the run will reduce the amount of wire and work necessary.

Ducks should have water for drinking throughout the day and in a container deep enough for them to completely immerse their heads. This water will require regular changing to keep it fresh. Always keep the ducks locked up until 9.30 or 10 am by which time most (if not all) of the eggs will have been laid. Letting the ducks out too early may mean eggs being laid in the run and these will quickly get soiled or damaged. Fruitless hours can be spent searching for the eggs from free-range ducks, so keep *them* locked up in the morning too.

Feeding

Ducks eat about 25 per cent more food than hens, and no duck is going to lay well without the right food. Like hens, ducks need a properly balanced diet with the right amounts of protein and vitamins. Even if the ducks have access to large areas of grassland they will still require supplementary feeding with a proprietary balancer ration.

Cooked potatoes, swedes, carrots and kitchen left-overs like old bread, cake and pudding waste, can account for up to half the daily ration of a layer fed a proprietary layers' mash or pellets in addition. Other useful foods are cooked onions, parsnips, cabbage, sprout leaves, lettuce, chickweed, dandelion leaves, beans and pea leaves. Avoid feeding anything that is slightly mouldy. Other things to avoid include salty dinner plate scrapings, citrus peel, banana skins, tea leaves, coffee grounds or mouldy meat and fish.

Layers' mash is obtainable from corn merchants and can be mixed with scraps of cooked potatoes, or whatever is available, into a crumbly mash. Do not make the mash too thin. The ratio should be about 1 lb of mash to 3 lb of cooked household waste. The laying duck needs a total of about 10 oz of food a day, given in two meals, one immediately after being locked up in the evening but slightly later than that in summer.

Pellets instead of mash can be fed dry twice a day, together with suitable kitchen left-overs, or ad-lib from a hopper. Meat and fish bones can also be rendered down and added to the feed. The food is best contained in troughs positioned near the water container because ducks like to wash their bills during meal times. Like hens, ducks also need flint or granite grit to retain in the gizzard for the food grinding process. They also need limestone or oyster shell grit (or crushed egg shell) to provide lime for egg shells.

Some proprietary feeds contain the necessary limestone, so check with the supplier. If there is any doubt, provide a container with a mixture of both, as with hens. Having the feed trough in the run may attract wild birds so put it just inside the house. The water trough can remain in the run.

What Breed to Buy?
The choice is between ducks that lay lots of eggs and those that fatten up well for the table. Whatever you decide, go to a good breeder. The top layers are the Khaki Campbell and the Welsh Harlequin and good table birds include the Aylesbury, the Muscovy and the Rouen.

a. Khaki Campbell duck

Khaki Campbell: Once the supreme layer until the Welsh Harlequin was developed. The Khaki Campbell was bred in 1901 by crossing an Indian Runner with a wild Mallard and later adding some Rouen blood. The ducks average 300 white eggs a year but generally make poor mothers. Khaki Campbells are poor as table birds, the meat is said to be 'stringy'. Mature drakes are khaki with a lighter colouring underneath and a bronze green head and neck; the ducks are completely khaki with slight darkening on the head and wings. Mature drakes reach 5 lb and ducks about $\frac{1}{2}$ lb less. The breed is widely available.

Welsh Harlequin: Possibly the best dual-purpose breed and of Khaki Campbell stock. The Welsh Harlequin originated in the U.K. in 1949. It also averages 300 white eggs a year but makes a better table bird than the Khaki, and can be ready for the table

b.Welsh Harlequin duck

at sixteen weeks, giving an oven weight of about 4 lb. Drakes get up to 7 lb and ducks, but the ducks are poor mothers. The Whalesbury, a hybrid, is the result of crossing a Welsh Harlequin duck with an Aylesbury drake. It is one of the leading commercial hybrids and a good dual-purpose breed with an average of 290 eggs a year.

Aylesbury: As a table breed the Aylesbury, which originated from the town of the same name, is unequalled because of its size and the rapid growth of ducklings. However, as a layer, it is not in the race with between 70 and 100 eggs a year. Drakes can weigh up to 10 lb and ducks 9 lb. Its plumage is white. For breeding purposes the ratio is one drake to four or five ducks. The breed is widely available.

c. Aylesbury duck

Indian Runner: Characterized by an almost upright stance, Indian Runners were first introduced into Britain from Malaya in about 1870. They are very hardy and although not large (about 4 lb for both drakes and ducks), the flesh is of good quality. Before the appearance of the Khaki Campbell it was the top laying breed averaging 180 a year. The breeding ratio is one to four and there are five varieties – black, white, fawn and white, fawn and chocolate. It is a good breed for smallholders because of its foraging ability.

Rouen: Another hardy breed which lays a greenish-blue egg, although not many of them, about 90 a year. The Rouen, which originated in France, makes a good table bird with drakes reaching 12 lb and ducks 10 lb. Breeding is one drake to three ducks. The plumage is similar to that of the Mallard from which most domestic ducks are descended.

d.Pekin duck

Pekin: Originally imported from China during the 1870s, the Pekin is sometimes crossed with the Aylesbury drake to produce a dual-purpose (eggs/meat) bird. It is good for the table by itself, though, with drakes getting up to 9 lb and ducks 8 lb, and averaging about 120 eggs a year. The breeding ratio is one drake to six ducks. The plumage is a uniform cream.

Muscovy: A good table bird with drakes reaching 14 lb and ducks 7 lb, the Muscovy originated from South America. It is normal to breed with one drake to six ducks, and the ducks make very good mothers who will hatch and rear their own eggs, a job which seems to be beyond the capabilities of most ducks. Plumage is black and white.

Orpington: A dual purpose bird bred from the Indian Runner, Rouen and Aylesbury. Ducks, which weigh about 7 lb (almost the same as the drakes) lay an average of 230-240 eggs a year. For breeding, use one drake to four ducks.

Cayuga: One of the 'ornamental' breeds and originating from the U.S.A., the Cayuga makes an acceptable table bird with game-flavoured meat, but as a layer the breed is not in the race. The ducks, however, can make excellent mothers. Plumage is a greenish-black.

Rearing

Whether you are keeping ducks for laying or drakes for the table, the rearing is the same for the first four weeks. Ducklings need heat for the first three weeks and this can be provided either by a broody duck (or a broody hen) or by using some form of artificial brooder. This can be a sophisticated purpose-built brooder, or something much simpler like a box filled with straw or hay and an infra-red bulb. In a warm room an ordinary light bulb will do suspended at a sensible distance above the ducklings (see page 112 in the chapter on geese).

If you have a broody duck or a broody hen, then use either or both, giving them a separate batch of ducklings each. The foster mother will have to be in a shed free of draughts and safe from rats, cats, dogs and all other enemies, and separate from any other hens or ducks. Litter the shed floor with peat moss, sawdust or well-chopped straw, and change this regularly because ducklings (and goslings too) are great splashers and the litter will get wet quickly.

Before introducing the ducklings to their foster mum let her sit on dummy eggs for four or five days just to make sure she really is broody, and introduce the ducklings after dark.

Place one of the ducklings beneath her and leave the two alone for twenty minutes before letting her have the rest at ten minute intervals, removing any dummy eggs at the same time. A duck can take a dozen ducklings but if she is sitting on fertile eggs instead let her have nine or ten. Bigger breeds like the Muscovy seem to make a better job of fostering than the lighter breeds but there are exceptions to every rule. Another 'ornamental' breed, the Black East Indian, is very much on the small side but the ducks can make very good mothers. Broody hens in fact will do the job as well as any duck and they are certainly less clumsy with the ducklings, and less likely to take them on long walks before they are ready which can result in deaths through exhaustion and over-exposure to bad weather. Sometimes ducks appear to have no instinct for the conditions ducklings can tolerate.

If neither a broody duck nor hen are available then the youngsters will have to be reared artificially. Day-old ducklings need a temperature of 85°-90°F/30°-32°C, which can be reduced by two degrees a day after the first few days. This in a 'hay box brooder' is achieved by raising the height of the lamp. Watch the ducklings and make sure that they are comfortably warm.

After ten days, if the weather is warm, artificial heat can be discontinued, but in cold weather let them have another four or five days of heat. It will not be necessary for the foster mother to remain with her brood for more than three weeks, and in warm weather ten to fourteen days will probably be quite long enough.

Feeding Ducklings
Ducklings can be fed on bread and milk, bread crumbs, biscuit crumbs and hard boiled eggs finely chopped up, but it is far easier to use a proprietary brand of starter crumbs. They are more expensive than doing-it-yourself but at least you know that the ducklings are getting the right start in life. Feed the crumbs dry and ad-lib in shallow containers, but do not use any feeders with slippery, glazed surfaces – like saucers – because the ducklings could slip and injure themselves. Some crumbs can be scattered among the litter on the shed floor. Finding the food will provide a useful exercise for the youngsters. Finely chopped greenstuff can be fed as well and a fresh supply of drinking water is vital.

Finely ground soluble and insoluble grits are needed from the first week. If the ducklings are with a foster mother then make sure she gets enough food too. After a few days, if the weather is warm enough, the ducklings can go outside in a grassland run for a few hours at a time. The run should have wire on top to foil any crows looking for an easy meal. Food and water containers should also be outside when the birds are in the run. Ducklings grow at a very rapid rate, and at four or five weeks, maybe earlier, they can be transferred to new housing giving a minimum of 3 sq ft each, and an adjoining grassed run. Their diet can also be changed to a growers' mash fed wet or dry three or four times a day.

Instead of mash, pellets can be fed ad-lib in containers that require filling only once a day. This may be less trouble and can result in better growth rates. At four weeks a well-reared duck can be almost half way to its nine-week killing weight of 7 lb.

Ducklings should not be allowed near swimming water until they are eight weeks old, so make sure that the water troughs are the right size for drinking and not big enough for swimming. At twelve to fourteen weeks the ducks can come off growers' rations and onto layers'. Food for laying hens will do and will probably be more easily available than duck rations. Ducks come into lay at between sixteen and twenty weeks, depending on the hatching date, and when at point-of-lay, each duck needs about 3 to 4 oz of layers' pellets or mash a day, together with the supplementary feed mentioned earlier and the necessary grit. If they are not free-ranging then take the greenfood, finely chopped, to them, but if they start leaving any reduce the amount.

Most eggs are laid during the hours of darkness or in the early morning. Collect the eggs regularly. They are larger than hen eggs, heavier and have a higher nutritional value. Unlike hens, ducks do not need extra winter lighting to keep production going when the days get shorter, which is another point in their favour. Egg production will, however, drop during the moult which comes any time after August, and the ducks will need to be fed well during the six-week moult. While moulting is taking place production may drop from an egg a day to one every two or three days but it will increase again once the moult is finished.

Some ducks are better layers than others. A good layer is a busy and active duck impatient to get at the food trough in the morning and an enthusiastic forager during the day. She may even look a little scruffy and down-at-heel. Ducks that are in immaculate condition are generally inferior layers, and poor layers which are not earning their keep should be culled and despatched to the freezer.

Table Birds
Properly reared table ducks can reach a decent weight for killing

in nine or ten weeks, sometimes less in the case of Aylesburys, so a good start is essential with plenty of high protein food.

Crumbs or pellets are expensive but the ducks will do better on them than home-made alternatives like bread and milk and boiled rice. Proprietary foods contain all the essential ingredients to promote growth, but do-it-yourself foods tend to be a bit hit-and-miss. Feed chick crumbs for the first month at two to three hour intervals, and after that switch to a growers' mash. At that stage it may be possible to reduce feed costs with cooked kitchen scraps.

While fattening, feed them as much as they will eat three times a day. Good fattening foods include: barley meal, ground crushed oats, small amounts of maize, stale bread (soaked overnight) boiled rice, cake and biscuit waste, skimmed milk, cooked fish scraps and greens. The more they eat the more weight they put on especially if they are in a run. Don't feed any food that smells stale or has begun to decompose. There are limits to what a fattening duck will eat. As with chickens (and geese) ducks are best starved during their final twelve hours so that the crop and intestines are empty of food when the end comes.

Killing

This is done by dislocating the neck where it joins the head in much the same way as killing chickens. Hold the duck by its feet with your left hand so that its head is hanging down; take the head in the right hand with the palm on the top of the head and the thumb against the underside of the neck and jerk the head firmly and quickly with the right hand to dislocate the neck. Correctly done this results in the breaking of the jugular vein and the blood drains from the veins in the body into the neck. An alternative method is to use a broomstick placed across the back of the duck's neck, as with killing geese.

Pluck the bird while it is still warm, when the feathers will come out more easily, and there is less danger of the skin getting torn. Hold the bird by the legs with the head hanging down to pluck and, as with hens and geese, do the job outside, in a garage or shed, but not in the house. Keep the feathers either for stuffing pillows or for the compost heap. Begin plucking at the tail and continue with the back, neck, wings, sides, legs and breast, leaving half the neck unplucked. Rough plucking like this will reveal the duck down which is a very boring job to remove. It is a question of simply sticking at it bit-by-bit but one way to speed the job up is to wrap the rough-plucked bird in a damp cloth and smooth it over with a warm iron, a bit like pressing a pair of trousers. When the cloth is taken off, the down and any feathers left after rough plucking come away with it – in theory at least. This method may also work with geese.

After plucking is complete clean up the feet and legs and hang the bird for a few days in a cool room free of houseflies. Hanging improves the flavour. Prepare ducks for the oven in the same way as with chickens.

Diseases

In the main, ducks are healthy creatures and subject to fewer diseases than chickens. Sensible precautions will keep most troubles at bay. Ducklings (and goslings) can get sunstroke because of the thin covering over their skulls, so make sure that they have adequate shade during the middle of the day when the sun is hottest. Sunstroke can prove fatal, and affected ducklings will be found on their backs kicking feebly. Frequently they do not recover. Adult ducks are not normally affected because their feathers offer protection from the sun's rays.

Good management of the house and run, and the avoidance of mouldy litter will eradicate most problems associated with parasites.

Two troubles that may arise are virus hepatitis and prolapse. Virus hepatitis is highly infectious and often proves fatal within two or three days. Birds that are affected by the virus go off their food, their walking movements become unco-ordinated and they fall on their sides kicking weakly. After two or three days some may recover but others may die. If the disease is suspected call in the vet so that he can take preventative action with vaccines which may protect others ducks in the flock.

Prolapse can affect ducks in the same way that it affects chickens and part of the internal organs may protrude while the duck is trying to lay or after she has finished. As with hens, wash the vent area gently with slightly warm water and try to push the organs back with one finger. Vaseline might help. Having pushed it back, isolate the duck for a few days and reduce her food to stop egg production for a while. If the trouble recurs often the only sensible alternative is to wring the duck's neck.

With luck you will not be faced either with prolapse or virus hepatitis. More troubles are likely to arise from physical causes than from disease. Ducks are not built for speed so when shepherding them into their house at night (unlike hens they may not go in of their own accord) do it slowly and gently. Do not rush round waving arms in all directions. If ducks are chased around they may get leg troubles or even collapse through over-exertion.

Breeding

For successful breeding a pond is desirable and is in fact essential when dealing with the heavier breeds like the Aylesbury as mating on land can lead to a ruptured drake. The ideal situation is a pond which is fed and drained by a natural stream, but most householders do not have running water in their back gardens so some sort of compromise is necessary. Ponds can be bought pre-formed in plastic or concrete, and are obtainable from garden stockists. If you do not want to go to that expense, a simple pond can be made by burying a bath or a galvanized water tank in the garden. Anything big enough and watertight will do, but half a dozen ducks will appreciate something larger than an old sink. You could try digging out a hollow and lining it with heavy-gauge plastic sheet and hope that the ducks will not start pecking holes in the lining.

Whatever you decide, remember that the water has got to be kept clean which might mean draining the pond with a syphon tube or baling out the water with buckets before re-filling.

For your own supply of fertile duck eggs you will need a drake and three or four ducks. Ducks are not mature enough for mating until they are about eight months old and drakes a month or two older – but it is best to use ducks that are eighteen months old. The drake should be with the ducks for at least four weeks before any eggs are taken for hatching purposes. The incubation period for duck eggs is anything from twenty-eight to thirty-four days.

10

GEESE

Like ducks, geese cannot be kept in a small back garden. They need space and a lot of good grass, and if you have both then you are very lucky because geese make good companions.

Seven geese are said to eat as much grass as one cow. That is an often-quoted comparison and proving it might be difficult, but it does underline the fact that geese are persistent grazers, which rules them out completely in the limited space available in the average garden. If, however, you have more space than that available, say at least a quarter acre of good grass, then geese merit serious consideration. Again check any local regulations and possible reactions from neighbours.

Geese are fine birds for the smallholder to have about the place. They live for a very long time, they rarely get ill if kept properly, they lay huge eggs of about 7 oz each and they look and taste good into the bargain. They are in fact easier to keep than hens. Certainly they seem to possess a greater intelligence. There are stories of geese said to be still laying when upwards of fifteen years and to be still alive and kicking at the age of forty. Certainly they can be long-lived but the average lifespan is probably nearer fifteen years. Geese can become fine and gentle companions. We once had a gander who spent hours grazing alongside a Jersey cow. Every morning he plodded off to see his friend and over the years they seemed to strike up a happy relationship slowly moving over the grass together.

There are a lot of myths too about the viciousness of geese — breaking people's arms with their wings and gouging out great lumps of flesh with their beaks. The worst you are likely to get is an almost apologetic nip now and then. Geese are not territorial fascists ready to maim anyone that comes within pecking distance. The males (ganders) will certainly take action to protect their wives if they think danger threatens, and two ganders, jealously proud of their respective harems, can have some right old punch-ups, especially during the spring when the geese are laying.

Because they are cheaper to feed than dogs they are sometimes used by security firms to scare off burglars. The Chinese goose is particularly effective, but kept domestically and handled with patience, love and care, geese can be endearing creatures. Nevertheless, geese, like hens and ducks, have got to pay their way and, realistically, the main attraction of keeping geese is that they can be fattened for the table almost completely on grass.

Feeding the young goslings some good 'starter' food is necessary to get them going at first but at two to three weeks, around April, they can be having their first bite of grass and after that they will keep growing.

When grass growth begins to slow down at the end of September their time is up. Geese killed by 29 September, the feast of Michaelmas, are known as Michaelmas geese. Taking the birds on a little longer and killing near Christmas will require additional food like barley, oats or a mixed grain if they are to put on significantly more weight.

Although geese can live and put on weight almost exclusively on grass the quality of the grass has got to be right. It is not much good putting six geese into an untouched jungle of coarse tufts and expecting them to fatten up and turn the place into a bowling green in the process. Geese can be good lawn mowers but they have their limits. Geese need short grass, so if it is too long then run the mower over it first. Nor should geese be put to graze on land which has been treated with insecticide. Incidentally, if you are a smallholder with a housecow she won't want to graze on land where geese have recently been because of the amount of droppings.

The goose has lost its popularity as a table bird partly because it is generally thought to be too fatty. This is true to an extent although goose fat does have its uses in cooking. Some people use it in baking. If the birds are killed off at the right time the fat content problem is largely overcome. Keeping the birds on too long in the hope of putting on more weight increases the risk of there being too much fat.

Two breeds, the Roman and the Chinese, can be killed earlier than other breeds because both mature quicker and the build-up of too much fat is thus overcome. The Chinese can be killed at eight weeks, although some of the smaller geese produce little more meat than a well-reared Aylesbury duck.

The laying season of the goose starts in February and if all goes well you should, in theory, be having your first egg by Valentine's Day. Geese lay far fewer eggs than hens and most breeds of duck. The lighter breeds like the Chinese and Roman lay more – up to sixty in the case of the Chinese – than heavier breeds like the Embden and Toulouse.

Fertile eggs can be incubated to produce new stock or hatched with a broody hen or goose although because the eggs are twice the size of hen eggs a broody hen can sit on only four or five. A broody goose will cover twelve to fourteen. You may also be able to exploit a market for goose eggs or use them yourself in omelettes. To use goose eggs in cooking though does seem something of a waste. It is much more profitable to incubate them to produce replacement stock or goslings for sale. But if you really want to use them for cooking they do make very good cakes and sponges. They are, however, a trifle too large for the breakfast egg cup.

All in all if you have the space of your own or have access to someone else's ground then give geese a try. A pond is not essential. Geese do not need to swim at all; all they want is a container of water deep enough for them to cover their heads completely. But I have always provided a pond – geese do enjoy a good swim and splash about.

Housing for Geese

Goose housing is much simpler than that for chickens since geese do not perch at night and do not require special nesting boxes. Like ducks, however, they are prone to cramp and rheumatism so a house with a dry floor, weather-proof roof and walls, and free from draughts is essential. Provided these criteria are met, almost any shed or outbuilding can be used. Concrete or rammed earth floors should be covered with a good four inches of litter – chopped straw, wood shavings or peat moss. The house should provide 5 sq ft for each bird. Geese, like ducks, will show their dislike of unsuitable housing by being very reluctant to enter at night. They can be persuaded to go in with a lot of arm-waving but it is far better to improve the accommodation. Use tongue-and-groove boarding on a stout wooden frame if you are building from scratch.

Most people who keep geese today have them free-ranging but if space is limited a pair of geese should not be kept on an area much less than 30 ft x 30 ft and even in a pen of that size will require most if not all their food to be provided. On the other hand two geese would live happily and find most of their own food on a quarter acre of good grass, although requiring supplementary feeding from late autumn onwards.

If the grazing area needs fencing this will need to be about 6 ft high with a 1 in mesh to keep foxes out. The fox is an ancient enemy of the goose. Special nesting boxes are not necessary because geese usually lay in rough nests in the corners of the house and follow a wild, protective instinct by covering the eggs with litter after leaving the nest. If the geese are free-ranging and laying outside, the nests may be difficult to find partly because of this cover-up operation and partly because geese do not always choose dark corners for laying like hens. Often the goose nest may be right out in the open in the most unexpected spot like the top of a dung heap. Keep an eye out to watch where the nests are, otherwise you may lose a lot of potentially valuable eggs. A goose in the process of laying advertizes her presence with a lot of cackling when approached and if the geese are with a gander he will often hang around each of his wives in turn until they have finished laying.

Which Breed?

Choosing which breed to acquire is far simpler than the choice for hens because there are only a handful of different breeds of goose. Commercially, geese have gone through a decline in popularity as table birds (only about 100,000 find their way onto the kitchen table each year in Britain compared with about 7 million turkeys at Christmas alone) and have not been 'improved' with selective breeding in the way that hybridization has produced an egg-laying machine from the humble hen.

Of the various breeds of geese, the Embden and the Toulouse are regarded as 'heavy breeds' which take longer to mature than the lighter breeds like the Chinese and Roman but the process of rearing the goslings is much the same.

Embden: recognized by its white plumage and bright orange legs, feet and bill; ganders weigh up to 30 lb and geese about 10 lb less. Although top of the weight table the Embden lays fewer eggs than other breeds – between thirty and forty a year. Embdens are frequently crossed with another of the heavy brigade, the Toulouse, and most of the geese seen wandering around farmyards in Britain are crosses of these two breeds.

Toulouse: another 'heavy' goose, the Toulouse has a dark, grey head and breast with a lighter shade on the thighs. The feathers on the wings and back are edged in white and the bill, legs and feet are orange.

Chinese: The earliest maturing breed, the Chinese comes in two colours, white and brown and the white is often said to look more like a swan than a goose. If space is limited the Chinese may be the best choice. It can be killed at eight weeks with good feeding. Males can grow up to 12 lb and females about 10 lb. The Chinese is also a champion laying breed with up to sixty a season and makes a good burglar alarm too.

Roman: Like the Embden a pure white bird. Ganders have a top weight of 15 lb and females 13 lb. One of the better laying breeds, the Roman, averages about forty-five eggs a season and is sometimes crossed with the Embden.

Brecon Buff: Generally recognized as one of the quieter breeds which could be a factor in their favour if there are neighbours nearby. The Brecon Buff is in the medium weight range with ganders of up to 19 lb and geese 3 lb less. Legs, feet and bill are pink and the plumage is not unlike that of the Toulouse.

Rearing Goslings

Some of these pure breeds may not be generally available in all areas so the easiest thing may be to go for an established cross like the Embden–Toulouse or the Embden–Roman. Check the small ads in the paper, or even insert your own 'geese wanted' advertisement. Goslings are normally available from such advertisements any time from mid-April onwards when they will be two weeks old and able to survive without artificial heat.

The simplest course of action might be to forget all about the breed and buy whatever goslings are available – they will probably be Embden–Toulouse anyway – with the idea of fattening some for the table and keeping perhaps three or four females to make up a breeding set for future years, which will mean buying an unrelated gander of a known breed later on. If the goslings are not old enough to survive without heat when you get them, then some kind of brooder will be needed. One way of doing this is in a haybox with heat supplied by an infra-red lamp. A haybox for six goslings can be made using a wooden box 3 ft square half filled with hay. The goslings will push the hay to the sides of the box making a warm bunker for themselves in the middle. Over the top at a height of about 15 in is hung a 100 watt infra-red bulb. If the apparatus is in an already warm room, like a centrally heated kitchen not subjected to great temperature fluctuations the infra-red bulb can be dispensed with and replaced with a normal light bulb.

If you are dealing with a greater number of goslings, say fifty, then a circular pen will have to be made of cardboard about 18 in high. The wattage of the bulb will need to be greater – perhaps 250 watts – and the apparatus will need to be set up in some suitable place indoors. The temperature for day-old goslings needs to be kept at between 85°-90°F/30°-32°C and lowered by two degrees a day after the first few days. If the temperature is too low the goslings will tend to huddle together in groups. If they remain against the cardboard perimeter then it is probably too warm.

Dry wood shavings can be used as litter in the circular pen and some dry hay will help insulation. At all times the litter needs to be kept dry which may mean regular changing.

Water drinkers should be placed as far as possible away from the heat source because dehydration can be fatal to young stock.

In both the haybox and the cardboard brooder, equipment for feeding and drinking can be fairly simple at first. For a few goslings the lid from a tobacco tin makes a good feeder and the bottom half a suitable drinker. Using saucers is not a good idea because glazed surfaces are too slippery and a gosling which slips and breaks a leg is not worth keeping. Casualties can be reared successfully but the job does demand a great deal of time, trouble and patience.

Goslings drink a lot of water in the early days but they seem to enjoy playing in it even more. They will probably splash it all over the place which means regular replacement of litter. They may even succeed in tipping the food and water containers over. Try putting a stone in both. After the first few days the tin lid feeder and drinker will have to be replaced with something bigger – either bought or home-made.

For the first three weeks goslings should be fed chick starter crumbs ad-lib whatever the breed. If for any reason you cannot get starter crumbs feed a mixture of hard boiled egg finely chopped up and mixed with breadcrumbs and softened with a drop of water. Chick crumbs though are better and less work.

After about a week, and assuming the weather is fine, put the goslings out in a small grass run for a few hours each day. The run should have a wire covering to keep out crows and rooks who will make off with a gosling or two given half a chance. Remember to transfer feeders and drinkers outside too. At three weeks old the goslings can be transferred permanently to an outside wire run (assuming they are not being allowed to free-range) and the amount of food can be reduced.

Keep the housing large enough for the number of geese (about 5 sq ft each) and simple – dry, weatherproof and fox-proof. Keeping foxes out is as important as giving shelter to the geese. If fattening the birds for the table, do not give them too much space or they will run off the weight gained. Do not cram them into a miserably small area though. Give them a good size run but never more than twelve birds to the quarter acre.

The larger breeds like the Embden and Toulouse (or the cross breed of both) can be kept on chick crumbs up to eight weeks only and then changed to growers' crumbs for another month. They do not have to be kept on chick crumbs for that length of time but the larger breeds do seem to require better feeding than the lighter ones. The lighter breeds can go on to growers' at four weeks and then on to mixed corn at twelve weeks. If, however, there is plenty of good quality, short grass, supplementary feeding can be stopped at around eight weeks and the birds can start grazing in earnest. Additional greenfood, like chopped cabbage and lettuce, can also be provided. For fast growth though feed each bird 2 to $2\frac{1}{2}$ oz of mixed corn a day.

Killing for the Table

Grass growth begins to slow down during August and September. However lush the grass might look at that time the essential protein content is declining so the geese can either be killed then or taken on further and killed before Christmas, although this will mean extra feeding of barley meal or mixed grain to compensate for the lack of protein available naturally.

Geese for the table are best killed when ten months old at the most. After that the meat tends to be very tough and rubbery. Geese being fattened up for Christmas should be kept off the pond – if there is one – in icy weather because when swimming they lose body heat to the water using up food which should be making meat instead. For the final two to three weeks the birds can be penned tightly or even kept indoors in a shed with an open front covered with wire netting and fed barley meal ad lib. Chopped greenfood can also be provided and is in fact essential if the birds are confined indoors.

As with hens and ducks, do not feed geese for the final twelve hours so that the last meal has cleared the gut. Killing is done by dislocating the neck but instead of pulling the head as with hens, the legs of the goose are pulled instead and, properly done, this results in instant death.

This is what you do: Hold the bird by its legs and wing tips (so that it cannot flap) and lower the head to the ground. The bird will then automatically bend its head back with its chin still resting on the ground. Get someone else to put a broomstick or something similar across the back of the neck, place your feet on the stick either side of the neck and, still holding the bird by the legs, give a sharp, upward pull and you will feel the spine in the neck break. The secret is in pulling hard enough to dislocate the neck without pulling the head off which makes for a very messy state of affairs with blood everywhere.

Plucking is best done as soon as possible while the body retains some warmth although some people hang the bird for at least twelve hours before plucking and claim this makes plucking even easier. Even for the experienced, plucking a goose can still be a tediously long job. Old clothes are a must and since goose down gets everywhere do the job outside or in a outbuilding but never indoors unless you happen to love house cleaning.

One possible alternative is to pluck the goose wet. Wet feathers do not blow about but you may get pretty wet yourself. Tie string around the leg of the goose and drop it into water of 82°F/28°C for five seconds making sure it is completely covered. Remove the bird and the feathers should come out easily when plucking starts.

Whether dry or wet plucking take all the feathers off as with chickens and then repeat the sequence to remove the down which can be kept for cushions or pillows. Any down remaining can be singed off using a lighted taper. Some people hold the bird over a gas jet; others flick it over with a blow lamp. The flavour of geese and ducks can be improved by hanging for a few days or even up to a week in a cold room.

Remember when working out how much meat you are likely to get that there is a lot of difference between a liveweight goose and the amount of usable meat produced. An 11 lb goose may not produce much more than 3-4 lb of meat.

Breeding Geese

Geese are best mated when they are two years old and not before. An unrelated gander is needed and you might have to hunt around for one of the right breed to mate with your remaining geese.

If you know of a local smallholder who breeds geese – possibly the person who supplied your original goslings – then go back to him for advice on obtaining a gander or failing that get a list of breeders from the British Waterfowl Association.

The generally accepted ratio is one gander to three geese of the heavier strains and one-to-four in the lighter weights. While a pond is not necessary for fattening geese for the table it is certainly desirable for breeding purposes. Most sexual relations between a gander and his wives seem to take place on water.

Breeding geese are reared in the same way as those being fattened and at eight weeks old can do without supplementary feeding if there is enough good grass about. When the quality of the grass starts declining in August and September, supplementary feeding will again be necessary. Feed crushed oats, mixed corn or wheat during the winter months, as much as they will clear up in ten minutes. The geese will always appreciate greenfood too from the garden and any kitchen leftovers like mashed potato. Don't overfeed maize though because its high (65 per cent) carbohydrate content is unhealthy for breeding stock and can lead to fewer eggs, reduced fertility rate and a disappointing success rate at hatching. The same applies if too much wheat is fed by itself, so resist the temptation of feeding wheat only, just because it is cheaper than most other feedstuff.

Each goose should be having 4 to 5 oz of crushed oats or a mixture of oats and mixed corn by the start of the laying season in the spring. For hatching, the eggs of mature birds are better than those from younger stock. Collect the eggs daily (although first find your nest if the geese are free-ranging!) and mark them with the date. Regular collection of the eggs encourages the goose to lay more.

Goose eggs can be kept for up to ten days before being set in an incubator or under a broody hen or goose. During this time they should be laid on their sides in sawdust or dry earth and turned each day to stop the yolk settling to the side which could kill the embryonic germ.

The period of incubation varies from twenty-eight to thirty-one days. In theory, hatching under a broody goose is the easiest because she will sit on ten or a dozen eggs, keeping them moist by taking regular trips to the pond. In practice though, not all breeds of geese go broody. It is dangerous to generalize but most Chinese do not and most Romans do at some stage. Embden and Toulouse do go broody some years but cannot be relied on. A sitting goose must be protected against rats and foxes. Rats are the worse menace. They will pull the eggs out from beneath a sitting goose and will also make a quick job of killing any newly-hatched goslings. Another problem is that after perhaps two or three weeks of patient sitting the broody goose may suddenly decide to leave her eggs to go stone cold for no apparent reason other than boredom with sitting around apparently doing nothing.

The snags do not end with the arrival of the newly hatched

goslings. Sometimes the gander may become steamed up with jealousy over the amount of attention his wife is giving to the goslings and kill them all by twisting their necks.

You could try instead placing fertile goose eggs beneath a broody chicken or bantam, both of which can make excellent foster mothers. The drawbacks are that a hen or bantam will only manage to cover perhaps half a dozen goose eggs and neither will be aware of the necessity of moistening them with water every day so you will have to do this yourself. All in all with the degree of risk involved – and the fact that the goslings may be worth £1 each as soon as they are hatched – the safest course of action is to put the eggs in an incubator.

An incubator is a worthwhile investment and with successful hatchings will pay for itself in a few years. Properly looked after it will not lose much in value either if you ever want to sell it.

When incubating goose eggs though do not expect to get 100 per cent returns. Returns of above 90 per cent are frequent with hen eggs but are nearly impossible with goose eggs partly because the correct degree of humidity is more critical. If the success rate is around 65-70 per cent then count yourself lucky since 50 per cent is much more common.

Surplus goslings can be sold at almost any stage from one day old onwards through an advertisement in your local paper, in fact the earlier the better because that means less work for you. Find out what any other people are charging before fixing your own price. Goose eggs can also be sold and if your local grocer or butcher is not interested in taking them then advertise them yourself. They should be worth around 25p apiece.

Goose Diseases

Thankfully these are very few since geese are healthy and hardy birds in the right surroundings. One problem you may come across is gizzard worm which causes most of the deaths in geese of all ages. Gizzard worm is a parasitic worm arising from over use of the same pasture. It leads to a serious loss of weight amongst goslings and older stock. Geese affected by the parasite which lives in the gizzard go off their food and may remain standing still on the same spot instead of grazing with the other birds. To break the worm cycle, grazing areas should be rested but keeping the geese off areas with long grass will reduce the likelihood of the stock picking up the disease. Regular worming of geese as advised by the local vet is a sensible precaution.

GLOSSARY OF TERMS

Addled: A fertile egg in which the embryo has died after starting to grow.

Air sac: The space at the broad end of the egg which supplies the growing embryo during incubation.

Albumen: The white of the egg as distinct from the yolk (ova).

Bantam: Small-scale breeds of hens which cost less to keep than full-size hens but which lay fewer eggs.

Battery: Intensive system in which hybrid hens are kept in wire cages for one or two years. Table birds ('broilers') are also housed and fattened in batteries.

Blood spot: Blood in the yolk or egg white caused by slight rupturing of blood vessels during formation; harmless both to eater of the egg and the layer.

Brooder: Heated device for the artificial rearing of young stock.

Candling: Method of determining whether fertile eggs are developing during incubation by shining a light through the egg; also used for checking quality of eggs for sale.

Capon: Cockerel which has been given a hormone pellet to make it put on weight more rapidly. The pellet, inserted under the skin, causes the bird's testes to shrink.

China eggs: Dummy eggs, also known as pot eggs or crock eggs, placed beneath a hen to check for broodiness.

Cock: Male bird of twelve months or over.

Cockerel: Male bird of under twelve months.

Comb: Fleshy tuft on the head of a fowl, especially the cock.

Clutch: Number of eggs that, in the natural state, a hen lays before deciding to sit; now refers to the number the poultryman lets her sit on for hatching.

Crop: Bag in the gullet where food is stored.

Crop-bound: Clogging up of the crop through bits of grass, straw or hay.

Cross-bred: Result of crossing two different breeds as in Rhode Island x Light Sussex hens and Embden x Toulouse geese.

Culling: Term applied to the removal of poor layers from the flock.

Debeaking: Cutting part of the beak to prevent feather pecking among hens; normally carried out by a vet using electric trimmer to remove and cauterize part of the beak; *not a job for the amateur.*

Deep-litter: Term applied to the keeping of hens under cover on clean straw, or shavings several inches deep.

Drake: Male duck.

Dual-purpose breed: Breed of hen, goose or duck, that lays well and provides a good carcass.

Dust bath: A box or depression in the ground filled with sand, sawdust or dry earth in which hens keep cool and clean.

Egg eating: Habit of some hens to eat their own eggs and the eggs from other hens often through boredom.

Feather pecking: Practice of some hens to peck feathers from other birds caused partly by idleness, overcrowding or poor diet.

Fowl: Collective term for chickens, geese and ducks.

Fowl Pest: Notifiable disease of hens also known as Newcastle disease; now less common.

Free-range: System of allowing fowl complete freedom to pick up available food as well as that provided.

Gander: Male goose.

Gizzard: Part of the digestive system in hens, ducks and geese where food is ground up.

Goose: Female of the species.

Gosling: Young goose or gander.

Grit: Insoluble material retained in gizzard to aid digestion; soluble limestone for calcium needed in forming egg shell.

Hen: Female bird which has passed through first laying season and is over twelve months old.

Hybrid: Hens bred from two or more breeds to produce lots of eggs.

Incubation: Process of producing young stock from fertile eggs either naturally or artificially.

Litter: Material covering floors of fowl houses.

Moult: Natural process of shedding old feathers and growing new ones.

Oviduct: Tube where eggs are formed.

Perch: Pole with rounded edges on which hens sleep (roost).

Pure bred: Hens, geese and ducks with the blood of only one breed in them; opposite of cross-bred.

Pullet: Chicken less than one year old.

Point of Lay: Pullet just about to start laying for first time.

Sex linkage: Union of two pure breeds which produce chicks of such colour and marking that the sexes are dissimilar when hatched.

USEFUL ADDRESSES

British Egg Information Service
  (part of the Eggs Authority)
37 Panton Street,
London SW1Y 4EW

British Waterfowl Association
25 Dale Street
Haltwhistle
Northumberland
NE49 9QB

Poultry Club of Great Britain
Honeypots Farm
Gusted Hall Lane
Hawkwell
Hockley
Essex.

Poultry World
Surrey House
Throwley Way
Sutton, Surrey.

Practical Self-Sufficiency
  (bi-monthly)
Editor: Mrs Katie Thear
Broad Leys Publishing Company
Widdington
Saffron Walden, Essex CB11 3SP

Ministry of Agriculture (Publications)
Tolcarne Drive
Pinner
Middlesex HA5 2DT
(advisory leaflets on hens, geese and ducks)

National Farmers Union
Agriculture House
Knightsbridge
London SW1X 7NJ

Chickens Lib
6 Pilling Lane
Skelmanthorpe
Huddersfield
West Yorkshire

R.S.P.C.A.
Manor House
The Causeway
Horsham
Surrey

INDEX